# 21-Day Clean-Eating Meal Plan - 1200 Calories

## Healthy Clean Eating Recipes: The 3-Week Weight Loss Cookbook for Beginners

### By Karla Bro

Disclaimer

All material in "21-Day Clean-Eating Meal Plan – 1200 Calories" is provided for your information only and may not be construed as medical advice or instruction. No action or inaction should be taken based solely on the contents of this information. Consult appropriate professionals for your health and well-being.

Remember that cooking is subjective. You may not achieve the results desired due to different brands of ingredients or different cooking abilities. Make sure you are not allergic to any ingredients.

I am not a chef. I'm just a person who likes cooking and writing about home-cooked food. Most of my recipes are created based on personal taste.

# Table of Contents

# Introduction

Someone said that clean eating means abstaining from all processed food or eating only raw food. But this isn't true. Clean eating means rejecting products with a high degree of processing (fried products, chips, sweets). It is the consumption of whole, minimally processed (and even better generally unprocessed) food (brown rice, fruits, and vegetables). Instead of focusing on using a certain number of food groups (for example, fewer carbohydrates and more protein), the idea of pure nutrition revolves around being attentive to food processing. The focus in a clean diet is the consumption of whole foods in their natural (if possible) or least-processed state, in which a significant amount of nutrients are retained during processing.

There are many problems associated with highly processed foods: excessive weight gain, the risk of cardiovascular diseases. Products with a high degree of processing don't have the nutrients necessary to maintain your overall health. Most of what you get from these foods are "empty" calories without the right amount of protein and trace elements. The result of this diet is a lack of nutrients, which predisposes you to various diseases.

Clean nutrition has many advantages.
**HELPS GET RID OF EXTRA WEIGHT**, as documented by several studies. Lack of calories with a balanced diet allows your body to switch from fat storage mode to burning mode.

At the same time, there is no deficiency of nutrients and no constant feeling of hunger because, in such food, there is a high content of micronutrients and protein. Protein is an essential nutrient for weight loss. It not only accelerates your metabolism but also reduces hunger. Additionally, more soluble fiber is in whole foods. Soluble fiber has many health benefits, one of which is increased weight loss.

**REDUCES THE RISK OF CANCER DEVELOPMENT.**
Studies have shown a positive correlation between nutrition and the prevention of various types of cancer, including breast cancer and colon cancer.

**REDUCES THE RISK OF HIGH BLOOD PRESSURE AND HEART DISEASES.**
These diseases are usually associated with high levels of bad cholesterol, but this problem can be eliminated by merely switching to a clean diet.

**IMPROVES IMMUNITY.**
By eating 5 or more servings of fruits and vegetables per day, the body's immune response can be improved up to 82 percent.

**IMPROVES SKIN CONDITION.**
Do not spend hundreds of dollars on cosmetics. Whole foods contain large amounts of antioxidants, healthy fats and other nutrients that play a huge role in skin health.

Clean Eating Rules

Shopping

First, go to the grocery store and pay attention to the signs in the produce section about how far your fruits, veggies, meat, and fish had to travel to reach you. Read nutrition labels, and don't choose products with unknown ingredients. Instead, try to pick foods without boxes, cans, bags, and packaging. All food must be fresh.

Cooking

Cook at home and you will know all about salt and sugar in your meal. Don't use high-fat cooking methods, such as deep-frying or stewing with animal or vegetable fat. You can steam, bake, or grill. Use olive oil; replace salt with garlic, spices, herbs, and lemon.

*Whole Grains and Natural Sugars*

Try to complete your meal with whole grains. Choose legumes and beans. They will be useful for your heart. Natural sugar must be in your meal plan. Use honey, maple sugar, or dehydrated sugar cane juice. There is no fat, cholesterol in the organic sweeteners.

You can eat the following:

· Single-ingredient grains (farro, oats, barley, brown rice, quinoa, millet, and amaranth)
· Whole-wheat pasta
· Popcorn
· Sprouted whole-grain bread
· Whole-wheat pizza dough

*Protein*

Don't forget about protein, a vital muscle-builder. It's essential in the first part of the day. Make sure to eat proteins at breakfast and lunch. Clean proteins are these:

- Chicken breasts and legs, ground beef
- Seafood, such as salmon and Pacific cod
- Eggs
- Unflavored nuts, such as almonds, hazelnuts, cashews, and walnuts
- Plain nut butter without sugar
- Dried beans

*Fruits and Vegetables*

These products are always a clear choice. Don't worry about sugar content. It's hard to overdo it. Tasty fruits and useful vegetables contain a lot of fiber, vitamins, and minerals.

It's better to limit your consumption of fruit juice because even 100% fruit juice doesn't contain the beneficial fiber of the whole fruits.

It's better to choose these:

- Fresh fruit
- Canned fruit without sugar
- Frozen fruit without sugar
- Dried fruit without sugar

Vegetables are the building blocks of clean-eating meals. They contain a lot of vitamins, minerals, and fiber. Canned and frozen vegetables are healthy too, but choose ones without sauces and read the labels.

Choose these vegetables:
- Any fresh vegetables
- Frozen and canned vegetable without sauce or salt.

*Dairy*

It's better to choose nondairy alternatives than dairy products. Choices are coconut, soy, and almond milk. If you like dairy products use regular or Greek yogurt, choose unsweetened varieties and low-fat products. Whole-milk dairy is the best choice.

Choose the following:
- Plain yogurt
- Milk
- Cheese
- Unsweetened nondairy milk

## Eat 5-6 times a day

This is the usual plan for healthy eating: three main meals and two to three snacks. This will prevent you from overeating while maintaining your blood sugar levels.

## Drink Right

Don't drink high-calorie drinks, such as specialty coffees, soft drinks, and vitamin waters. It's better to choose clean water or unsweetened tea. Organic milk and 100% fruit juice with sparkling water are also clean drinks.

## How to Transitions to a Clean Diet

1. The decision should be well thought out and not just emotional. So, determine the reason and tell yourself, "That's

why I turned to clean food, and I am not going to turn off my intended path!"

2. Allocate time. Sit down and think about how much time you can devote to a new lifestyle. You may have to spend an extra hour a day preparing a healthy lunch.

3. Goals should be simple and measurable. If you love cookies, telling yourself, "I will eat fewer cookies" is abstract. While saying, "I will eat one cookie a day" is more specific, it is better to say, "Instead of cookies, I will eat fruit."

4. Get rid of harmful products. List all your favorite "harmful" products. You need to throw away artificial, ultra-processed foods from your refrigerator and pantry.

5. Replenish your stocks with "clean" products. Gradually replace harmful products with clean products. Start with fruits and vegetables. Then include wholegrain food in your diet.

6. Start your day with a clean breakfast. Fruit and green smoothies are a good option. Eat this way for 1-2 weeks and you'll develop the desire to eat clean lunches and dinners.

7. Do not eat when you are full. Do you not know proper portions? Then, stop eating when your stomach is full.

8. Study labels, and choose products with natural ingredients.

9. Get to know your local farmers. They will be able to supply you with independently grown, organic products.

10. Start cooking.

11. Drink 1.5 to 3 liters of water per day. Water normalizes all processes in the body.

12. Adhere to the clean food plan.

## Count the Calories

If you want to lose weight, reduce your number of calories and increase your physical activity. If you wish to lose 1 to 1 ½ pounds per week, reduce your calorie intake by 500-750 calories:

- A diet with 1200 to 1500 calories per day is safe for women;
- A diet with 1500 to 1800 calories per day is safe for men and women who exercise regularly.

Don't use low-calorie diets of fewer than 800 calories per day. You can only eat in this way if your doctor is monitoring you.

We made the meal plan for 21 days and used a 1200-1300 calorie diet menu. You can combine meals and ingredients to taste and complement the menu for the day. Also, increase portions if you want to cook for the whole family.

We recommend this menu for 1 to 6 people.

# Week 1 Diet Plan

| MEAL | Breakfast | | Lunch | | Dinner | |
|---|---|---|---|---|---|---|
| | **Week 1** | | | | | |
| SUNDAY | Avocado Egg Toast | | Minestrone (slow cooker) | | Tuna Green and Egg Salad | Salmon and Asparagus with Onion-Mushroom Sauce |
| MONDAY | Almond Banana Shake | | Clean Eating Fried Rice with Chicken | | Grilled Salmon with Lemon | Fresh cherry tomatoes |
| TUESDAY | Roll-Up Omelet with Spinach | | Quinoa Enchilada Bake with Cheese | | Peach Rice Bowl with Shrimp | |
| WEDNESDAY | Avocado Chicken Roll | Cucumber Cocktails | Pasta Salad with Mozzarella, Pesto, and Tomatoes | | Chicken and Vegetable Skewers | Braised Beef and Zucchini |
| THURSDAY | Marinara Poached Egg | | Grilled Shrimp and Avocado | | Phyllo Cups with Vegan Potatoes and Olive | |
| FRIDAY | Pita Pocket Sandwich | | Warm Barley Chickpea Tomato Salad | | Grilled Salmon Kebobs with Lemon | |
| SATURDAY | Sesame Edamame | Grilled Chicken Breast | Chicken Lettuce Cups | Chocolate Pudding | Turkey Rolls with Vegetables | |

Avocado Egg Toast
Minestrone (slow cooker)
Tuna Green and Egg Salad
Salmon and Asparagus with Onion-Mushroom Sauce
(1215 calories)

# Breakfast

## Avocado Egg Toast

271 calories per person|1 serves | 15 min

*Ingredients*

¼ avocado

¼ tsp ground pepper

1/8 tsp garlic powder

1 slice toasted whole-wheat bread

1 large boiled egg

1 tbsp sliced scallion

*Direction*

1. Take a small bowl. Combine avocado, garlic, and pepper in it gently.
2. Top the toast with avocado mixture.
3. Cut into half the egg. Place the egg on a top of the toast.
4. If you want to garnish the toast with the scallion.

## A.M. Snack

1 medium orange (62 calories)

# Lunch

## Minestrone (slow cooker)

240 calories per person | 1 serves| 3-6 h

*Ingredients*

1/6 small onion, diced

1/6 stalk celery, diced

1/3 carrot, peeled and sliced

1/3 zucchini, sliced

1/3 potato, peeled and cubed

1/3 cup green beans (fresh or frozen)

1/6 cup peas (fresh or frozen)

1/3 cup kale, coarsely chopped

1/3 cup vegetable broth or water (for thinner Minestrone)

1/6 can (70 g) diced tomatoes with liquid

1/6 can (70 g) kidney beans, dried and rinsed

20 ml tomato or vegetable juice

1/6 tsp sea salt

a pinch ground black pepper

2 fresh basil leaves, minced

10 g Parmesan or Parmigiano Reggiano

*Direction*

1.  Place all the ingredients except kale, parmesan, and basil, in a slow cooker. Cover and cook 5-6 hours on low or 3-4 hours on high.

2.  When the minestrone is cooked, add the kale. Then, cook for 5 minutes on high.

3.  Serve minestrone in the bowls and drizzle with olive oil. Sprinkle the dish with fresh basil and Parmesan.

AND

# Tuna Green and Egg Salad

164 calories per person | 1 serves| 20 min

*Ingredients*

3 oz canned tuna

1 oz lettuce

1 chicken eggs

1/4 medium onion

1/2 tbsp olive oil

lemon juice to taste

salt

*Direction*

1. Cut the lettuce and put it on the plate.
2. Open the can and remove the tuna. Cut pieces, if necessary.
3. Mince the onion, and put it on the fish.
4. Boil the eggs. Cut them in half lengthwise.
5. Season the salad with oil. Add a couple drops of lemon juice and salt.

# P. M. snack

1 medium kiwi (42 calories)

# Dinner

# Salmon and Asparagus with Onion-Mushroom Sauce

478 calories per person | 1 serves| 30 min

*Ingredients*

¼ lb salmon

1 oz champignons

¼ onion

¼-garlic clove

½ tbsp olive oil

2 tsp cup sesame oil

salt

basil

pepper

*Direction*

Marinade

Mix sesame oil with finely chopped garlic, basil, pepper, and salt.

Salmon and Asparagus

1. Cut the salmon, and put into a small saucepan. Pour the marinade over fish and chill in the refrigerator for an hour.
2. Preheat the oven to 355 °F. Cover a baking sheet with foil.
3. Put the slices of salmon and washed asparagus on the baking sheet. Cover them with foil.

4. Bake fish and vegetables in the oven for 15–20 minutes.
5. Wash, peel, and cut champignons. Mince the onion. Fry the ingredients in olive oil until browned.
6. Remove the fish and asparagus from the oven, and top with mushroom and onion mixture. Bake for another 10 minutes.

Almond Banana Shake
Clean Eating Fried Rice with Chicken
Grilled Salmon with Lemon
Fresh cherry tomatoes
(1171 calories)

# Breakfast
## Almond Banana Shake

450 calories per person | 1 serves| 5 min

*Ingredients*

½ cup silken tofu

½ cup milk (1%)

2 bananas

2 tbsp almond butter

2 tbsp hemp seeds

¾ tsp cinnamon

1 tsp vanilla extract

2 tbsp honey

1 cup ice

*Direction*

1. Place all ingredients in a blender. Do not use ice. Mix well.

2. Add ice and mix again.

3. Serve.

## A.M Snack

1 medium kiwi (42calories)

# Lunch

## Clean Eating Fried Rice with Chicken

266 calories per person | 1 serves| 50 min

*Ingredients*

1/4 cup long-grain brown rice

¼ cup water

a pinch of salt

1/6 tbsp olive oil

½ oz onions, chopped

1/6 cup diced red or green bell pepper

1/3 boneless skinless chicken breast

1 egg, beaten

½ tbsp soy sauce

1/6 tbsp ginger root, peeled and finely minced

1/3 tsp sesame oil

½ oz scallions (or green onion), chopped

*Direction*

1.    Boil water over high heat. Add rice and salt to boiling water. Reduce heat and cover pot. Cook for 30-40 minutes, until liquid is absorbed. Then, remove the rice from the heat. Refrigerate until cold.

2.    Add olive oil to a nonstick skillet or wok. Add sliced chicken, bell pepper, onions, and ginger. Cook for 5 minutes over medium heat.

3.    Add rice and remaining water. Cook over medium-high heat.

4.    Push rice to one side of the pan, and then add the beaten eggs to the free side. Scramble the dish quickly. Add

soy sauce and sesame oil. Cook for 3-4 minutes. Remove skillet from heat.

## P.M. Snack

1 tbsp cashew (55 calories)

## Dinner
## Grilled Salmon with Lemon

308 calories per person | 1 serves| 35 min

*Ingredients*

½ lb wild salmon

¼ lemon

½ tbsp extra virgin olive oil

¼ tbsp fresh squeezed lemon juice

1 tbsp fresh rosemary, minced

¼ tbsp Dijon mustard

1/2 clove garlic, minced

sea salt and black pepper to taste

1 bamboo or wood skewers, soaked in warm water for 30 minutes

*Direction*

1.   Heat the grill on medium heat. Spray the grates with olive oil.

2.   Mix oregano, lemon juice, mustard, fresh rosemary, garlic, and black pepper in a bowl.

3.   Cut salmon into cubes.

4.   Slice the lemon into thin rings.

5. Thread salmon and lemon slices onto the skewers, alternating between salmon and lemon. You should have about eight pairs.

6. Spray the kebobs with oil, spice mixture, and salt.

7. Grill the fish and lemon about 10 minutes, turning occasionally.

AND

**Fresh cherry tomatoes** (1/2 lb, 50 calories)

Roll-Up Omelet with Spinach
Quinoa Enchilada Bake with Cheese
Peach Rice Bowl with Shrimp
(1159 calories)

# Breakfast
## Roll-Up Omelet with Spinach

198 calories per person | 1 serves| 40 min

*Ingredients*

1 tsp canola oil

1 egg

1 cup baby spinach

1 tsp olive tapenade

1 tbsp crumbled goat cheese

*Direction*

1.  Drizzle canola oil into a nonstick pan. Then, wipe with a paper towel. Heat the pan over medium heat.

2.  Beat egg and swirl into the frying pan. Cook 2 minutes. Then, flip the egg and cook 1 minute.

3.  Carefully place the egg on a plate.

4.  In the same pan, sauté 1 cup of spinach about 1 minute, until wilted.

5.  Top the egg with olive tapenade and goat cheese. Then place wilted spinach on the ingredients.

6.  Roll up the egg and cut in half.

## A.M. Snack

1 medium orange (62 calories)

# Lunch

## Quinoa Enchilada Bake with Cheese

407 calories per person | 1 serves| 1 h

*Ingredients*

1/6 cup cooked quinoa

1 oz frozen corn

1 oz tomatoes, finely diced

½ oz black beans, drained

1/8 purple onion, chopped

½ oz jalapeno, seeded and diced

½ oz Enchilada Sauce

2 oz reduced fat cheddar cheese

½ oz chopped cilantro

½ oz black olives, sliced

½ oz avocado, diced

*Direction*

1.   Preheat the oven to 340 °F.

2.   Combine quinoa, corn, one cup of the tomatoes, beans, onions, jalapeno, enchilada sauce, and 1 cup cheddar cheese in a large bowl. Place the ingredients into a 2-quart baking dish.

3.   Top the dish with the remaining cheese. Sprinkle the dish with remaining tomatoes, the cilantro (without 1 tsp), and the sliced olives.

4.   Bake for 50 minutes.

5.   Remove from the oven and top the dish with 1 tsp cilantro and diced avocado. Add salt and pepper to taste.

## P. M. Snack

1 medium, 100 g banana (89 calories)

## Dinner

## Peach Rice Bowl with Shrimp

403 calories per person | 1 serves| 40 min

*Ingredients*

¾ cup uncooked brown rice

1 ½ low-sodium chicken broth (or use vegetable broth)

½ lb shelled large raw shrimp

1/2 firm, ripe peach, pitted and chopped

¼ clove garlic, peeled and sliced

a pinch of saffron threads (optional)

a pinch of paprika

a pinch of sea salt

¼ tbsp fresh lime juice

1 oz cilantro leaves, coarsely chopped

½ tbsp extra virgin olive oil

¼ lime, cut into four wedges

*Direction*

1.  Add the broth and rice to a pot and bring to a boil. Cover the pot and cook for 35 minutes, until liquid is absorbed and rice is tender. Fluff with a fork.

2.  Toss chopped peaches with a half of lime juice. Set aside.

3.   Heat sauté pan over medium heat. Add olive oil, then shrimp, salt to taste, paprika, cayenne pepper, and saffron. Cook for 3 minutes.

4.   Add garlic. Cook for 1 minute, until shrimp are pink and opaque. Then, remove the pan from heat.

5.   Remove the rice to a bowl. Add shrimp and peaches and sprinkle the dish with the cilantro.

6.   Serve with lemon wedges if desired.

Avocado Chicken Roll
Cucumber Cocktails
Pasta Salad with Mozzarella, Pesto, and Tomatoes
Chicken and Vegetable Skewers
Braised Beef and Zucchini
(1201 calories)

# Breakfast
## Avocado Chicken Roll

397 calories per person | 1 serves| 15 min

*Ingredients*

4 oz fried chicken breast

1 tbsp mayonnaise

½ medium avocado, 3 oz

salt

pepper

*Direction*

1. Cut the chicken into thin long strips.
2. Cut avocado into medium slices, put them in a plate, mix with mayonnaise and salt and pepper to taste.
3. Put avocado mixture on the meat strips. Roll strips.

# A.M. Snack
## Cucumber Cocktails

104 caloriesper person | 1 serves| 10 min

*Ingredients*

1-cup buttermilk

2 cucumbers

fennel

salt

pepper

*Direction*

1. Finely chop cucumber.

2. Chop the dill. Mix the ingredients with buttermilk.

3. Add salt and pepper to taste. Drink immediately after preparation

# Lunch
# Pasta Salad with Mozzarella, Pesto, and Tomatoes

285 calories per person | 1 serves |25 min

*Ingredients*

2 oz whole grain short pasta

3 fresh basil leaves

1/4 tbsp pine nuts

1/4 clove garlic

salt to taste

1 tsp extra virgin olive oil

¼ cup cherry tomatoes, halved or quartered

1 tbsp Parmesan flakes

1 oz Mozzarella

*Direction*

Pesto

In a blender, combine nuts, basil, garlic, salt, and Parmesan.

Pasta

1. Boil pasta, cooking according to the package directions until al dente.

2. Rinse pasta with cold water and drain. Place in a bowl and drizzle with about 1 tbsp. extra virgin olive oil.

3. Mix the pasta with the pesto. Add tomatoes and Mozzarella.

AND

# Chicken and Vegetable Skewers

113 calories per person | 4 serves | 25 min

*Ingredients*

3 lb chicken breast

1 small eggplant

1 bell pepper

1 zucchini

1 big red onion

16 basil leaves

3/4 tsp salt

1/4 ground pepper

4 tbsp balsamic vinegar

*Direction*

1.   Slice chicken breast to 1-1/2 inch-wide strips. Rub with 1/2 tsp salt, 1/2 tsp pepper.

2.   Cube an eggplant, slice the bell pepper, zucchini, red onion. Rub them with salt and pepper.

3.   Thread the chicken and vegetables to the skewers.

4.   Grill until cooking through.

5.   Before serving, drizzle chicken and vegetables with balsamic vinegar

# P. M. snack

1/2 medium orange (82 calories)

# Dinner
# Braised Beef and Zucchini

302 calories per person | 1 serves| 1 h 30 min

*Ingredients*

1/3 lb beef

3 oz zucchini

½ onion

1 tbsp olive oil

salt

pepper

*Direction*

1. Cut beef and onions into small pieces.
2. Put the olive oil in a frying pan, and add the beef and onions. Fry until golden brown on high heat.
3. Add a little water, cover and stew for one hour on low heat.
4. Cut the zucchini into slices. Add the vegetables and spices to the beef and stew for 30 minutes.

Marinara Poached Egg
Grilled Shrimp and Avocado
Phyllo Cups with Vegan Potatoes and Olive
(1361 calories)

# Breakfast
## Marinara Poached Egg

306 calories per person | 1 serves| 15 min

*Ingredients*

2 tsp olive oil

¼ small yellow onion

A pinch of red pepper flakes

½ cup marinara sauce

1 egg

1 small whole wheat pita pocket

*Direction*

1.   Heat the olive oil in a small sauté pan over medium heat.

2.   Sauté the onion in the pan until brown, approximately 5 minutes.

3.   Add red pepper flakes and marinara sauce. Cook about 1 minute.

4.   Gently break the egg into the pan. Cover the pan and simmer about 5 to 7 minutes until egg white is firm.

5.   Serve the dish with pita pocket. You can toast it and tear it into wedges.

## A.M. snack

1 medium apple (65 calories)

# Lunch

## Grilled Shrimp and Avocado

393 calories per person | 1 serves|30 min

*Ingredients*

3 oz shrimp

salt to taste

black pepper to taste

1/6 tbsp onion powder

1/6 lemon

1/3 tbsp coconut aminos

1/3 tbsp avocado oil

1/3 ripe Hass avocados

*Direction*

1. Peel and clean the shrimp. Place them in a bowl.
2. Add salt, coconut aminos, pepper, onion powder. Add the juice of one half of the lemon. Combine.
3. Heat the grill or frying pan. Add avocado oil. Place shrimp in pan and cook for 3 minutes. Flip the shrimp.
4. Remove the shrimp and cool.
5. Peel and mush avocado with the fork. Add a little salt and lemon juice.
6. Put avocado mixture and the shrimp on the plate

# P.M. snack

1/2 medium banana (30 calories)

# Dinner
## Phyllo Cups with Vegan Potatoes and Olive

567 calories per person | 1 serves|25 min

*Ingredients*

½ lb potato

1 tbsp extra virgin olive oil

¼ tbsp nutritional yeast

Salt (kosher)

¼ medium shallot

½ tbsp red wine vinegar

1/4 tsp tomato paste

sweet smoked paprika to taste

cayenne to taste

a pinch of parsley

1/2 large bell peppers

3 olives

7-8 mini phyllo shells

*Direction*

1.    Clean and peel the potatoes. Put in a small saucepan. Add water to cover potatoes.

2.    Boil the potatoes about for 10 minutes. Drain through a sieve.

3.    Retune the potatoes to the saucepan. Add 2 tbsp oil, the yeast, and ½ tsp of salt.

4.    Mash the potatoes with a fork, until only a few lumps remain.

5.  Preheat the frying pan with 2 tbsp oil.

6.  Add the shallots and a pinch of salt. Cook about 3 minutes until brown and soft.

7.  Add the vinegar, tomato paste, paprika, and cayenne.

8.  Cook until the spices are toasted and the oil turns brick red about 1 minute. Remove from the heat, and scrape every last bit into the mashed potatoes.

9.  Add half the parsley and peppers, the olives and 3/4 tsp salt. Stir to combine.

10.  Preheat the oven to 425 ºF.

11.  Arrange the phyllo cups on a baking sheet and fill each with the potato mixture. Bake until the filling is hot, 4 to 5 minutes.

12.  Garnish with the remaining parsley and peppers.

Pita Pocket Sandwich
Warm Barley Chickpea Tomato Salad
Grilled Salmon Kebobs with Lemon
(1191 calories)

# Breakfast
## Pita Pocket Sandwich

297 calories per person | 1 serves| 25 min

*Ingredients*

1 eggs

1 egg whites

½ tbsp milk

½ whole wheat pita pocket, cut in half

½ cup baby spinach

2 grape tomatoes, sliced in half lengthwise

1 green onions, diced

1/8 cup crumbles of Feta cheese

1 tsp olive oil

*Direction*

1.    Preheat oven to 340 °F.

2.    Whisk the eggs and egg whites with milk, tomatoes, and spinach in a medium mixing bowl. Add green onion, salt, and pepper to taste.

3.    Pour the mixture in a non-stick skillet.

4.    Cook the eggs for 15-18 minutes over medium-high heat. Sprinkle the top with feta cheese. Place in the oven for 1 minute.

5.    Brush each pita half with olive oil (both sides). Warm on the foil for 2 minutes.

6.    After baking, cut the omelet and place it on the pita.

## A.M. snack 7 almonds (50 calories)

# Lunch

## Warm Barley Chickpea Tomato Salad

402 calories per person | 1 serves| 45 min

*Ingredients*

1/8 cup uncooked barley

3 oz chicken fillet

1/4 tbsp extra virgin olive oil

1/8 cup cherry tomatoes, halved

1/4 cup pre-cooked chickpeas

¼ bunch of fresh sage

1/8 tbsp balsamic vinegar

Salt and pepper to taste

*Direction*

1.   Bring the barley to a boil in a pot with salted water. Then, cover and simmer on low heat for ½ hour, until tender.

2.   Drain and rinse barley. Set aside.

3.   Heat griddle to medium. Grill the chicken for 2 minutes per side. If chicken is thick, it may need to cook longer. Then, chop and set aside.

4.   Sauté the tomatoes in a saucepan with olive oil over medium heat. Cook for 1 minute.

5.   Add chickpeas, barley, and sage to tomatoes. Stir the ingredients for 5 minutes.

6.   Add the chicken. Cook for 1-2 minutes.

7.   Season the dish with balsamic vinegar, salt and pepper to taste. Cook for 1 minute.

8.   Eat warm.

## P.M. snack

1 medium pear (48 calories)

## Dinner
## Grilled Salmon Kebobs with Lemon

308 calories per serving | 1 serves| 40 min

*Ingredients*

5 oz salmon (or some other fish)

¼ lemon

½ tbsp extra virgin olive oil

¼ tbsp fresh squeezed lemon juice

1 tbsp fresh rosemary, minced

¼ tbsp Dijon mustard

1/2 clove garlic, minced

sea salt and black pepper to taste

1 bamboo or wood skewers, soaked in warm water for 30 minutes

*Direction*

1.  Heat the grill on medium heat. Spray the grates with olive oil.

2.  Mix oregano, lemon juice, mustard, fresh rosemary, garlic, and black pepper in a bowl.

3.  Cut salmon into cubes.

4.  Slice the lemon into thin rings.

5.  Thread salmon and lemon slices onto the skewers, alternating between salmon and lemon. You should have about eight pairs.

6.  Spray the kebobs with oil, spice mixture, and salt.

7.  Grill the fish and lemon about 10 minutes, turning occasionally.

AND

## Cucumber and tomato to taste, ½ lb

(86 calories)

Sesame Edamame
Grilled Chicken Breast
Chicken Lettuce Cups
Chocolate Pudding
Turkey Rolls with Vegetables
(1211 calories)

# Breakfast
## Sesame Edamame
156 calories per person | 1 serves| 10 min

*Ingredients*

1/2 tbsp water

3/4 cup edamame pods

1/3 tbsp light brown sugar

1/6 tbsp dark sesame oil

1/6 tbsp rice vinegar

kosher salt to taste

freshly ground black pepper to taste

1/4 tsp sesame seeds, toasted

*Direction*

1. Boil water in a large frying pan over medium-high heat
2. Add edamame to water. Cook 2 minutes.
3. Add sugar, vinegar, oil, salt, and pepper to edamame. Cook for 3-5 minutes.
4. Sprinkle with sesame seeds before serving.

## Grilled Chicken Breast
165 calories per person | 1 serves| 25 min

*Ingredients*

¼ lb chicken breast, skinless and boneless

¼ garlic clove

1/3 tbsp olive oil

rosemary, optionally

a pinch of smoked sweet paprika

salt and pepper to taste

*Direction*

1.    Place the chicken breast in a large bowl. Sprinkle it with olive oil, garlic, salt, and pepper. Stir with tongs and let sit for 10 minutes.

2.    Preheat the grill on medium-high to 450-500 ºF. Rub with the oiled paper towel.

3.    Place chicken on the grill, close the lid and grill for 8-10 minutes turning once. Don't overcook.

4.    Remove from the grill, cover with foil and let rest for 5 minutes.

## A.M. snack

1 medium banana (80 calories)

# Lunch

## Chicken Lettuce Cups

120 calories per person | 1 serves| 30 min

*Ingredients*

1/4 tbsp cooking oil

1/6 chicken breast, pound ground

1/3 shallots, diced

a pinch of red onion, diced

1/6 clove garlic, very finely minced

Fresh chiles, minced, to taste

1/6 tbsp fish sauce

1/8 lime, juiced

1/6 tsp low-sodium soy sauce

1/6 head iceberg lettuce, leaves separated into cups

1/6 handful of cilantro

Mint, cut into chiffonade, to taste

*Direction*

1.   Heat a wok over high heat. Or you can take large sauté pan. Swirl in oil. Add the chicken. Using a spatula, break up the meat, spreading out over the pan's surface. Cook about 3 minutes, until brown.

2.   Add the shallots, onion, garlic, and chiles to the remaining oil in the pan.

3.   Place the ground chicken on one side of the pan. Swirl in the garlic-onion mixture. Sauté about 30 seconds, until fragrant.

4.   Add the fish sauce, lime juice, and soy sauce to a pan. Cook for 1-2 minutes.

5. Cool the chicken.

6. Serve the chicken in the lettuce cups. Top with the herbs.

## Chocolate Pudding

220 calories per person | 1 serves|10 min

*Ingredients*

¼ medium avocado

1 tbsp cup honey

1/5 tbsp coconut oil

a pinch of pure vanilla

a few drops of balsamic vinegar

1 tbsp unsweetened cocoa powder

Pinch of sea salt

*Direction*

1. In a food processor, mix avocado, honey, coconut oil, vanilla, and vinegar. Pulse until smooth. Scrape the sides.

2. Add the cocoa powder and salt. Mix until pudding consistency. Serve.

## P.M. snack

5 pecan halves (50 calories)

# Dinner
## Turkey Rolls with Vegetables

420 calories per person | 1 serves| 35 min

*Ingredients*

4 oz turkey

2 oz cream cheese

¼ avocado

¼ bell pepper

¼ cucumber

¼ tbsp. olive oil

1/4 clove of garlic

lemon juice

salt

pepper

*Direction*

1.   Take turkey breast, if necessary, wash.

2.   Mix the lemon juice, chopped garlic, and pepper in a small bowl.

3.   Place the turkey in a deep bowl, pour it with the lemon mixture and leave it to marinate for two hours.

4.   Preheat the oven to 400 F.

5.   Place the turkey on a baking sheet, bake for 30 minutes in the oven.

6.   Cool ready meat.

7.   Put slightly softened cream cheese in a bowl. Beat it with a food processor.

8.   Peel the avocado. Mash it with a fork. Add a couple of drops of lemon juice, and salt.

9. Mix the avocado with the cream cheese. Add olive oil, whisk with a blender to the thick consistency.

10. Cut the pepper and cucumber into thin strips.

11. Slice thinly baked turkey. Each piece of meat smear with the cheese and avocado sauce. Place the pepper and cucumber on the turkey, roll them.

## Tomato and Bell Pepper Smoothies

50 calories per person | 1 serves| 5 min

*Ingredients*

½-cup tomato juice

½-cup carrot juice

1 bell peppers

½ tbsp lemon juice

ground black pepper

*Direction*

1. Wash, peel and cut peppers into medium-sized pieces. Place in a blender.

2. Add lemon juice and black ground pepper to taste. Add tomato and carrot juices. Beat.

3. Drink immediately after preparation◻

# Week 2 Diet Plan

| MEAL | Week 2 | | | | |
|---|---|---|---|---|---|
| | **Breakfast** | | **Lunch** | **Dinner** | |
| **SUNDAY** | Vegetable Salad with Nuts and Dried Fruits | Turkey Muffins with Mashed Potatoes | Cauliflower Gratin | Coconut Chicken Strips | |
| **MONDAY** | Roasted Veggie Frittata | | Vegan Sweet Potato and Kale | Soba with Honey Dressing | |
| **TUESDAY** | Almond Banana Shake | Herb-Crusted Turkey Breast | Carrots and Seaweed Vegetable Salad | Vegan Casserole Ratatouile | |
| **WEDNESDAY** | Banana-Oat Smoothie with Citrus | Chickpea Frittata with Potatoes and Kale | Carrot and Nut Cake | Tuna Salad from the Mediterranean | |
| **THURSDAY** | Vegan Pulled Pork Sliders with Coleslaw | Blueberries and Tofu Cheese Smoothies | Spring Rolls with Carrot Sauce and Herb-Crusted Turkey Breast | Creamy Mashed Potatoes with Cauliflower | Greek Salad |
| **FRIDAY** | Sunflower Granola Parfait | | Grilled Turkey Burgers and Cucumber Salad | Vegan Shepherd's Pie | |
| **SATURDAY** | Paleo Overnight Casserole | Quinoa Stir-Fry | Grilled Chicken Breast | Vegan Lasagna | |

Vegetable Salad with Nuts and Dried Fruits
Turkey Muffins with Mashed Potatoes
Cauliflower Gratin
Coconut Chicken Strips
(1237 calories)

# Breakfast
## Vegetable Salad + Nuts and Dried Fruits

410 calories per person | 1 serves | 20 min

*Ingredients*

¼ beetroot

¼ carrot

2-3 walnuts

2-3 dates

½ tbsp raisins

2 tsp honey

¼ bunch lettuce (3 oz)

1 tsp olive oil

*Direction*

1.  Wash and boil the beets and carrots. Cool, and then peel.

2.  Clean walnuts and break into medium pieces. Then, wash discard pits and, grind.

3.  Wash the raisins and lettuce. Place the dates on a deep plate and drizzle with vegetable oil.

4.  Then, add the honey and mix well.

5.  Put prepared raisins and walnuts on a plate.

6.  Cut beetroot and carrot into medium-sized pieces.

7.  Finally, add the chopped lettuce. Mix ingredients well. Add salt or spices as desired.⌧

# A.M. snack

½ mango (47 calories)

# Lunch

# Turkey Muffins with Mashed Potatoes

329 calories per person | 1 serves| 40 min

*Ingredients Muffins*

3 oz lean ground turkey

1/4 egg, beaten

1 tbsp whole wheat breadcrumbs

1 tbsp ketchup

2 tbsp onion, diced

1/8 carrot, grated

1 tbsp fresh parsley, finely chopped

1/6 clove garlic, minced

1/3 tsp Worcestershire sauce

kosher salt to taste

black pepper to taste

1/6 tsp dried oregano

*Ingredients_Mash*

1/2 large russet potatoes, peeled and chopped

1/6 tbsp extra virgin olive oil

1 tbsp low-fat milk

kosher salt to taste

*Direction*

1.  Preheat oven to 170 °C. Take a cup muffin tin. Spray it with cooking spray.

2.  Place the potatoes into a pot with cold salted water. Boil for 20 minutes, until tender. Then, drain the liquid and mash the potatoes with milk, olive oil, and salt.

3.  Mix ground turkey, breadcrumbs, ketchup, onion, carrots, parsley, garlic, Worcestershire sauce, salt, pepper, and oregano in a large bowl, using your hands. Divide the mixture into muffins cups. Each cup should be 2/3rds full. Bake for 35 minutes, until cooked through.

4.  Remove the muffins from the oven. Cool for 5 minutes. Remove the muffins from tin. Spread mashed potatoes over each muffin, making peaks if desired.

## P.M. snack

5 cashews (50 calories)

## Dinner
## Cauliflower Gratin

140 calories per person | 4 serves | 50 min
*Ingredients*
1 ½ lb cauliflower
1 tbsp vegan butter
1 tbsp chickpea flour
1 cups cashew milk
1/4 tsp kosher salt
black pepper to taste
Nutmeg, a pinch

¼ cup vegan cheddar cheese

2 tbsp gluten-free bread crumbs

1 tbsp vegan grated parmesan

1 tbsp extra-virgin olive oil

*Direction*

1.  Wash and cut into large florets the cauliflower.

2.  Boil water in a pot a few minutes. Place the florets in it. Blanche the cauliflower until tendering but with crunch.

3.  Drain and rinse the cauliflower with cold water.

4.  Preheat the oven to 400 ºF.

5.  Melt the butter in a medium-size saucepan. Add the flour until well combined.

6.  Add the warm milk. Whisk milk until a smooth sauce.

7.  Salt and pepper. Add the nutmeg, cheese. Whisk the ingredients until smooth. Turn off the heat.

8.  Put a part of the béchamel sauce in the bottom of baking sheet (8x8-inch).

9.  Combine the bread crumbs, oil and parmesan. Mix them. Sprinkle them over the cauliflower.

10. Bake for 30 minutes. Turn the oven on broiler for a few minutes for crisp up the top.

AND

# Coconut Chicken Strips

261 calories per person | 4 serves | 35 min

*Ingredients*

1 lb boneless skinless chicken breasts

2 tbsp extra virgin olive oil

¼ tsp pepper

½ tsp salt

1 cup unsweetened coconut flakes (or use shredded coconut)

## Soy-Ketchup Sauce

½ cup ketchup

2 tbsp lite soy sauce

2 tbsp water

¼ tsp pepper

*Direction*

1. Preheat the oven to 200 °C.

2. Slice the chicken into strips. Coat the chicken with olive oil.

3. Mix salt, pepper, and coconut in a bowl. Cover chicken with the mixture.

4. Place the chicken strips on the baking sheet. Bake for 30 minutes, until golden brown.

5. Serve the chicken with the sauce.

## Sauce

Mix the ingredients in a bowl.

Roasted Veggie Frittata
Vegan Sweet Potato and Kale
Soba with Honey Dressing
(1195 calories)

# Breakfast
## Roasted Veggie Frittata

139 calories per person | 1 serves|1h 30 min

*Ingredients*

1/2 medium bell peppers

1/2 garlic clove

1/3 large zucchini

1/6 medium onion

1/6 tbsp olive oil

1 tbsp cup fresh parsley, chopped

1 ½ eggs

1 egg whites

salt to taste

cayenne pepper to taste

2 tbsp finely shredded Parmesan

Nonstick cooking spray

*Direction*

1.   Preheat oven to 400 °F. Place the first oven rack in the lowest position. The second rack must be in the central position in the oven. Line two baking pans with foil. Spray the foil with cooking spray.

2.   Place bell pepper and garlic on one pan. Place zucchini and onion on the other baking pan. Brush the products with olive oil. Place zucchini and onion on the center rack and bake 15 minutes. Remove onion and zucchini.

3.   Place bell pepper and garlic on the lower rack. Roast for 10 minutes.

4. Peel the bell pepper and garlic. Cut pepper into quarters. Cut the zucchini into three 1/2-inch strips. Cut the onion into ½-inch slices. Chop the parsley. Shred the Parmesan.

5. Place the vegetables and garlic in a bowl. Add parsley and ½ tsp of salt.

6. Lower the heat in the oven to the 400 ºF. Coat a 9-x-1.5-inch round cake pan (or smaller) with cooking spray.

7. In a medium bowl, whisk eggs and egg whites. Add remaining salt and cayenne pepper.

8. Add egg mixture to the vegetable mixture. Stir in Parmesan. Place the ingredients into the cake pan.

9. Bake the mixture for 50 minutes.

10. Let the frittata stand 15-30 min before serving.

## A.M. snack

2 peaches (72 calories)

# Lunch
## Vegan Sweet Potato and Kale

667 calories per person | 1 serves| 30 min

*Ingredients*

1 ½ tsp olive oil

1 tsp cumin

1 cup finely chopped onion

1 cup finely chopped tomato

2 tsp ginger

1 tbsp and 2 tsp grated garlic

½ tsp ground turmeric

¾ tsp ground chili

1 ½ tsp ground coriander

2 cups kale

1 cups sweet potato chunks

1 ½ cups water

½-cup coconut milk

½ tsp garam masala (a combination of whole spices)

Salt to taste

*Direction*

1. Heat olive oil in the stockpot. Add cumin seeds.

2. Wait until the seeds crackle. Add onion. Cook on low heat until brown.

3. Add grated ginger and garlic. Fry the ingredients for 2 minutes.

4. Add tomatoes. Cook mixture until mushy.

5. Reduce heat to low and add chili, turmeric, and coriander. Fry for 3 minutes.

6.  Add ¾ cup of water. Raise heat to medium, and boil the ingredients.

7.  Wait until water is evaporated. Add sweet potato, kale, and salt. Stir for 3 minutes.

8.  Add 1 ½ cup of water. Mix the ingredients, and cook for 13 minutes until potato is cooked through.

9.  Add coconut milk and garam masala. Cook for 5 minutes.

10. Serve immediately after cooking.

☒

## P.M. snack

Two brazil nuts (65 calories)
½ medium orange (40 calories)

# Dinner
## Soba with Honey Dressing
212 calories per person | 3 serves | 20 min

*Ingredients*

2 tbsp lite soy sauce

1 tbsp rice wine vinegar

½ tbsp honey

1 tbsp sesame oil

1-inch ginger, peeled and grated

4 oz soba noodles

½ cucumber

½ endive

½ tbsp toasted sesame seeds

½ tbsp pine nuts

½ tbsp chives, finely chopped

*Direction*

Dressing

1.  Whisk the soy sauce, rice wine vinegar, sesame oil, honey, and ginger in a small bowl.

Salad

1.  Clean, peel, and slice the vegetables into small pieces.

2.  Boil water over medium-high heat. Add the soba noodles. Cook for 4-5 min. At first, drain the noodles. Rinse them with cold water. Drain again.

3.  Mix soba noodles, vegetables, sesame seeds, chives, and pine nuts. Top with dressing.

Almond Banana Shake
Herb-Crusted Turkey Breast
Carrots and Seaweed Vegetable Salad
Vegan Casserole Ratatouile
(1150 calories)

# Breakfast
## Almond Banana Shake

450 calories per person | 1 serves| 5 min

*Ingredients*

½ cup silken tofu

½ cup milk (1%)

2 bananas

2 tbsp almond butter

2 tbsp hemp seeds

¾ tsp cinnamon

1 tsp vanilla extract

2 tbsp honey

1 cup ice

*Direction*

1.   Place all ingredients in a blender. Don't use ice. Mix well.

2.   Add ice and mix again.

3.   Serve.

## A.M. snack

Two kiwi (50 calories)

# Lunch
## Herb-Crusted Turkey Breast

233 calories per person | 1 serves|1h 20 min

*Ingredients*

1 lb bone-in turkey breast (remove the skin before eating)

½ tbsp garlic powder

½ tbsp poultry seasoning

½ tsp dried thyme

1/8 tsp black pepper

½ tbsp onion powder

½ tsp olive oil

1 tbsp water

*Direction*

1.  Preheat the oven to 340 °F.
2.  Mix all spices in a small bowl.
3.  Cover entirely both sides of turkey breast with spice mixture.
4.  Drizzle the baking dish with olive oil and water. Add turkey breast and cover with the foil.
5.  Cook dish for 40-60 minutes.


AND


## Carrots and Seaweed Vegetable Salad

137 calories per person |1 serves| 20 min

*Ingredients*

2 oz carrots

2 oz pickled seaweed wakame

2 cherry tomatoes

1 tbsp soy sauce

1 tbsp water

½ tbsp sesame

¼ tsp lemon juice

¼ tsp sesame oil

¼ tsp sugar

¼ tsp cornstarch

*Direction*

Salad

1.  Wash and peel carrots. Then grate carrots with a medium grater.

2.  Mix wakame with grated carrots.

3.  Wash cherry tomatoes and cut in the halves. Add tomatoes to carrots and seaweed.

4.  Add salad dressing, stir, and garnished with sesame seeds.

Dressing

1.  Heat the water and add sugar.

2.  Thicken the mixture with starch.

3.  Add soy sauce, sesame oil, and lemon juice.

☒

# P.M. snack

10 cashews (50 calories)

# Dinner

## Vegan Casserole Ratatouille

139 calories per person | 1 serves| 1h 30 min

*Ingredients*

<u>For the Sauce:</u>

¼ large tomato

½ cloves of garlic

½ tbsp extra virgin olive oil

<u>For the Main dish:</u>

1 tbsp canned tomato puree

¼ large eggplant

¼ large green zucchini

½ large tomatoes

Olive oil or sunflower oil for baking

Sea salt and black pepper powder to taste

Fresh thyme

*Direction*

<u>Sauce</u>

1.   Wash and finely dice the tomato. Peel and chop garlic cloves.

2.   Preheat the frying pan. Add oil. Add tomatoes, garlic, and tomato puree.

3.   Mix and cook the ingredients until creamy, 10 minutes.

4.   Remove the pan from the heat. Add salt and black pepper to taste.

Ratatouille

1. Wash and slice eggplant. Season the slices with salt. Set aside the eggplant for 10 minutes.

2. Wash and slice the tomatoes and green zucchini.

3. Preheat the oven to 400 °F.

4. Sprinkle the bottom of a casserole dish with olive oil

5. Place tomato sauce in the dish. Then arrange the sliced vegetables in the dish in alternating patterns.

6. Sprinkle the ingredients with more olive oil.

7. Bake the casserole for 40-45 minutes.

Banana-Oat Smoothie with Citrus
Chickpea Frittata with Potatoes and Kale
Carrot and Nut Cake
Tuna Salad from the Mediterranean
(1321 calories)

# Breakfast

## Banana-Oat Smoothie with Citrus

228 calories per person | 1 serves| 5 min

*Ingredients*

2/3 cup fresh orange juice

½ cup prepared quick-cooking oats

½ cup plain 2% Greek yogurt

1 tbsp flaxseed meal

1 tbsp honey

½ tsp grated orange rind

1 large banana, sliced and frozen

1 cup cubed iced

*Direction*

1.  Place all ingredients in a blender. Mix well.
2.  Add ice and blend again.

# A.M. snack

raw walnuts 1 tbsp (53 calories)

# Lunch

## Chickpea Frittata with Potatoes and Kale

151 calories per person | 4 serves | 1h 30 min

*Ingredients*

1 ¼ cup water

1/3 cup chickpea flour

½ tsp smoked paprika

½ tsp fine sea salt

¼ tsp garlic powder

½ tbsp olive oil

1 cup chopped and peeled sweet potato

½ medium-chopped onion

2 cups chopped kale


*Direction*

1.   Preheat the oven to 350 °F.

2.   Whisk the water, chickpea flour, paprika, salt, garlic powder in a medium bowl.

3.   Heat olive oil in a cast iron skillet over medium heat.

4.   Add sweet potato, onion in a skillet. Cook for 10 minutes. Add the kale and cook for 3 minutes.

5.   Remove the vegetables in a frying pan from heat. Pour the chickpea flour batter.

6.   Place the ingredients in the heated oven. Bake for 50 minutes.

7.   After cooking cool the dish for 30 minutes before cutting.

# Carrot and Nut Cake

520 calories per person | 4 serves | 1h 10 min

*Ingredients*

2 oz almond flour

1 oz coconut flour

2 tbsp baking powder

2 oz pecan

1 tbsp chia seeds

4 oz grated carrot

4 chicken eggs

4 oz Philadelphia cream cheese

4 oz sour cream (30%)

3 oz butter

vanilla

cinnamon

salt

*Direction*

1.  Preheat oven to 320 ºF.

2.  Prepare the cream. In a blender, place the cream cheese, sour cream and vanilla to taste. Mix everything well until smooth. Allow the mixture to sit.

3.  Mix almond and coconut flour, chia seeds and pecans. Add baking powder, salt, and cinnamon. Grind all these dry ingredients in the flour. You can leave large pieces.

4.  Grated carrot.

5.  Separate the yolks in the eggs. Beat the eggs white to add air. Mix the yolks.

6. Melt the butter and let cool. Mix the egg whites with the yolks. Add creamy melted butter. Mix again.

7. In the mixture add dry ingredients: mix flour, nuts and seeds. Gently stir manually or with a blender.

8. Fold the carrots evenly into the batter.

9. Place the batter onto a baking sheet and bake in the oven for 45 minutes.

10. Cool the cake and cut into several layers. Smear each layer with cream. Let the cake rest overnight in the refrigerator.

## P.M. snack

papaya 4 oz (32 calories)

# Dinner

## Tuna Salad from the Mediterranean

337 calories | 2 serves | 10 min

*Ingredients*

½ can of tuna in spring water

¼ cup artichoke hearts, diced

¼ cup pitted Kalamata olives, chopped

¼ roasted red pepper, chopped

1 tbsp cup fresh parsley, chopped

1 tbsp basil leaves, slivered

1 ½ tbsp olive oil

½ lemon, juiced

Salt and fresh ground pepper to taste

*Direction*

1.  Take a big bowl. Place all the ingredients in it. Season with salt and pepper. Chill the salad before serving.

2.  Serve the dish with lettuce leaves, baguette, or whole grain crackers.

Vegan Pulled Pork Sliders with **Coleslaw**
Blueberries and Tofu Cheese Smoothies
Spring Rolls with Carrot Sauce
Herb-Crusted Turkey Breast
Creamy Mashed Potatoes with Cauliflower
Greek Salad

(1343 calories)

# Breakfast

## Vegan Pulled Pork Sliders with Coleslaw

95 calories per person | 6 serves | 1h 10 min

*Ingredients "Pulled Pork"*

3 tbsp vegetable oil

½ lb portobello mushrooms

1 tbsp soy sauce

½ tbsp molasses

½ tbsp brown sugar

a pinch of smoked paprika

¼ tsp garlic powder

kosher salt and ground black pepper

*Ingredients Coleslaw*

½ cup sliced green cabbage

¼ cup grated carrots

1/8 cup vegan mayonnaise

½ tsp cider vinegar

¼ tsp celery seed

Pinch sugar

Salt and ground pepper to taste

*Direction "Pulled Pork"*

1. Preheat the oven to 300°F. Place two baking sheets with parchment paper. Brush them with tablespoon of vegetable oil.
2. Take the third sheet or pan. Place it with paper towels.

3. Clean and slice mushrooms about 1/8-inch thick. Place the mushroom slices very close together on the parchment. Brush with the remaining vegetable oil.
4. Bake the mushrooms for 25 or 30 minutes.
5. Flip the mushrooms over; rotate the pans in the oven. Bake the mushrooms until well-browned and the edges are crispy, for 30 minutes.
6. Remove the mushrooms from the oven and transfer to the paper-towel lined baking sheet to dry for a few minutes.
7. Whisk the soy sauce, molasses, brown sugar, paprika and garlic powder in a large bowl.
8. Toss the mushrooms in the marinade, do this in several batches.
9. Return the marinated mushrooms to the baking sheets in a single layer.
10. Sprinkle the mushrooms with salt and a few grinds of pepper and return to the oven until crisp, 5 minutes.

*Direction Coleslaw*

1. Clean, peel and combine the cabbage, and carrots in a large bowl.
2. Mix the mayonnaise, vinegar, celery seed and sugar in a small bowl.
3. Add salt and pepper to taste.
4. Pour the dressing over the cabbage and carrots.
5. Add more sugar, salt and pepper to taste.
6. Chill before serving.

AND

# Blueberries and Tofu Cheese Smoothies

120 calories per person| 1 serves| 5 min

*Ingredients*

1 cup water

1 cup blueberry

2 oz tofu cheese

1 banana

handful of almonds

*Direction*

1.   Peel and cut the banana into medium slices. Place in a blender.

2.   Add blueberries, tofu and almonds. Add water and beat well.

3.   Drink immediately after preparation.

## A.M. snack

4 oz fresh cherry (48 calories)

# Lunch
## Spring Rolls with Carrot Sauce

186 calories per person | 6 serves |40 min

*Ingredients*

Spring Rolls

6 paper wrappers

6 lettuce leaves

1 medium carrot

1 cucumber

¾ cup daikon radish

1 red pepper without seeds

Sause

3 medium carrots

1 small shallot

2 tbsp grated ginger

¼ cup rice wine vinegar

2 tbsp low-sodium soy sauce

¼ tsp toasted sesame oil

salt and pepper to taste

¼ cup canola oil

¼ cup water

*Direction*

Spring Rolls

1.    Wash, clean and peel carrot, daikon radish. Chop them and cucumber, pepper. Place the vegetables in a bowl, mix them.

2.    Dip rice paper in a steaming hot water. Do this quickly. Lay wrappers on a flat surface.

3.   For one serves. Take 1 wrapper and place 1/6 mixture of vegetables in the center of it. Add lettuce leaf on top.

4.   Roll up one side, tuck in both edges, seal the roll.

5.   Continue with other 5 wrappers and other ingredients.

Dipping sauce

1.   Place carrots, shallot, grated ginger, rice wine vinegar, low-sodium soy sauce, toasted sesame oil, salt, pepper in a food processor.

2.   Mix all ingredients until smooth. Add canola oil, water. Blend well.

# Herb-Crusted Turkey Breast

233 calories per person | 3 serves | 1h 20 min

*Ingredients*

1 lb bone-in turkey breast (remove the skin before eating)

½ tbsp garlic powder

½ tbsp poultry seasoning

½ tsp dried thyme

1/8 tsp black pepper

½ tbsp onion powder

½ tsp olive oil

1 tbsp water


*Direction*

1.  Preheat the oven to 170 °C.

2.  Mix all spices in a small bowl.

3.  Cover entirely both sides of turkey breast with spice mixture.

4.  Drizzle the baking dish with olive oil and water. Add turkey breast and cover with the foil.

5.  Cook dish for 40-60 minutes.


# P.M. snack

2 oz avocado (85 calories)

# Dinner

## Creamy Mashed Potatoes + Cauliflower

324 calories per person | 6 serves | 20 min

*Ingredients*

½ lb riced cauliflower

½ cup sour cream

3 tbsp heavy whipping cream

3 tbsp butter

¼ tbsp garlic powder

4 tbsp Parmesan cheese

2 tbsp chopped chives

salt and pepper

*Direction*

1. Place the cauliflower on a deep plate, and cover with paper towel. Microwave cauliflower for 5 minutes. You can roast or steam it too. Cauliflower must be slightly soft.
2. Add sour cream, heavy whipping cream, butter, garlic powder, Parmesan cheese, salt, pepper to taste. Mix the ingredients with an immersion blender.
3. Add 1 tbsp of chopped chives to the mixture. Mix well.
4. You can serve the dish with mashed potatoes and 1 tbsp chives.

AND

# Greek Salad

252 calories per person | 4 serves | 30 min

*Ingredients*

2 ripe tomatoes

½ cucumber

½ red onion

½ green bell pepper

½ lb feta cheese

10 black olives

2 tbsp olive oil

½ tbsp red wine vinegar

2 tsp dried oregano

salt and pepper

*Direction*

Salad

1. Cut the tomatoes and cucumber into bite-sized pieces.
2. Thinly slice the bell pepper and onion.
3. Arrange the ingredients on a plate.
4. Add feta and olives.
5. Drizzle the salad with the dressing.
6. Sprinkle with oregano.

Dressing

Mix the olive oil and vinegar. Add salt and pepper to taste.

Sunflower Granola Parfait
Grilled Turkey Burgers and Cucumber Salad
Vegan Shepherd's Pie
(1268 calories)

# Breakfast
## Sunflower Granola Parfait

235 calories per person | 1 serves| 10 min

*Ingredients*

2/3 cup fresh orange juice

½ cup prepared quick-cooking oats

½ cup plain 2% Greek yogurt

1 tbsp flaxseed meal

1 tbsp honey

½ tsp grated orange rind

1 large banana, sliced and frozen

1 cup cubed iced

*Direction*

1. Place all ingredients in a blender. Mix well.
2. Add ice and blend again.

## A.M. snack

50 g avocado (85 calories)

# Lunch

## Grilled Turkey Burgers+ Cucumber Salad

314 calories per person |1 serves| 30 min

*Ingredients Turkey Burgers*

4 oz lean ground turkey

¼ whisk egg

1/8 cup plain whole wheat breadcrumbs (such as whole wheat panko)

½ tbsp onion, grated

¼ clove garlic, minced

kosher or sea salt to taste

black pepper to taste

¼ tbsp extra virgin olive oil

½ tsp canola oil or cooking spray

*Ingredients Cucumber salad*

½ small cucumber, diced

1/8 cup green onions, chopped

¼ ripe tomato, finely diced

½ tbsp squeezed lemon juice

kosher or sea salt to taste

*Direction*

<u>Burgers</u>

1.   Mix all ingredients, except olive oil. Form 4-5 patties. Sprinkle both sides of each patty with olive oil.

2.   Lightly coat grill with olive oil.  Set to medium-high heat.

3. Place patties on grill and cover. Cook for 5–6 minutes on each side.

Salad

1. Mix all ingredients. Chill until serving.

# P.M. snack

1 medium orange (82 calories)

# Dinner
# Vegan Shepherd's Pie

552 calories per person | 6 serves |1h 10 min

*Ingredients*

## Mashed Potatoes

5 russet potatoes (cut 1-inch cubes)

½ cup vegan mayonnaise

½ cup soy milk

¼ cup olive oil

3 tbsp vegan cream cheese

2 tsp salt


## For the bottom layer

1 tbsp vegetable oil

1 big yellow onion (chopped)

2 carrots

3 stalks celery

½ cup frozen peas

1 tomato

1 tsp italian seasoning

1 clove of garlic

1 pinch ground black pepper

1 lb package vegetarian ground beef substitute

½ cup Cheddar-style soy cheese


*Direction*

1.   Clean, peel, cut 1-inch cubes the potatoes. Place in a pot. Cover the potatoes with cold water. Boil the potatoes about 25 minutes. After that, drain it.

2.  Add soy milk, vegan mayonnaise, salt, olive oil, vegan cream cheese. Mush the ingredients well until fluffy. Use a potato masher.

3.  Preheat the oven to 400°F. Spray the baking sheet with cooking spray.

4.  Take the large frying pan. Heat the vegetable oil in it over medium heat. Place carrots, onion, frozen peas, celery, and tomato in it. Cook for 10 minutes until softened.

5.  Stir the vegetables with Italian seasoning, pepper, garlic.

6.  Reduce the heat to medium-low. Add the vegetarian ground beef substitute to the vegetables in the pan. Cook for 5 minutes.

7.  Spread the vegetarian meat substitute mixture into the bottom of the baking dish.

8.  Place the mashed potatoes on the vegetarian mixture.

9.  Shred the soy cheese. Spread mashed potatoes with the cheese.

10. Bake the casserole for 20 minutes in the oven.

Paleo Overnight Casserole
Quinoa Stir-Fry
Grilled Chicken Breast
Vegan Lasagna
(1355 calories)

# Breakfast
## Paleo Overnight Casserole

263 calories per person | 5 serves |1h 15 min

*Ingredients*

½ lb nitrate-free sausage

½ tsp garlic powder

¼ tsp thyme

¼ tsp sage

1/8 tsp crushed red pepper

½ onion, diced

2 sweet potatoes, peeled and cubed

½ green bell pepper

4 eggs

¼ cup coconut milk

salt and pepper to taste

*Direction*

This dish is time-intensive, but the taste is worth it. You must start preparing this dish the evening before.

1.   Preheat a large pan over medium heat. Cook sausage, stirring to crumble.

2.   Add spices, onion, green pepper, and sweet potatoes. Stir occasionally for 5-7 minutes.

3.   Remove pan from heat, and cool slightly.

4.   Spray baking dish with cooking spray. Use 9 x 13-inch dish. Spread the sweet potatoes and sausage mixture on the bottom of the dish.

5.   Whisk coconut milk with the eggs. Pour the mixture over sausage and potatoes.

6.   Cover the ingredients and refrigerate overnight.

7.   Next morning, turn on the oven and preheat it to 170 ºC. Cover casserole with foil, and bake for 35 min. Remove foil and bake an additional 10 minutes.

## A.M. snack

1 medium kiwi (42 calories)

# Lunch

## Quinoa Stir-Fry

269 calories per person | 3 serves | 30 min

*Ingredients*

½ tbsp extra virgin olive oil

1 tsp sesame seed oil

1 cloves garlic, minced

2 stalks bok choy, leaves removed and sliced into ½-inch pieces

½ cup broccoli florets

1 tbsp soy sauce

2 cups quinoa, cooked and chilled

1/8 cup toasted sesame seed


*Direction*

1.   Heat a large skillet on medium-low heat. Add sesame and olive oil, garlic. Sauté until fragrant, 1 minute.

2.   Add bok choy and broccoli to the skillet. Cover and cook 5 minutes, until slightly tender.

3.   Remove broccoli from the skillet.

4.   Add soy sauce, and cooked quinoa until heated through, stirring occasionally.

5.   Turn off the heat. Place broccoli on the top of quinoa. Sprinkle with toasted sesame seeds.

6.   Cover the skillet and let rest for 5 minutes.

7.   Eat warm.

AND

# Grilled Chicken Breast

165 calories per person | 1 serves| 30 min

*Ingredients*

4 oz chicken breast, skinless and boneless

¼ garlic clove

1/3 tbsp olive oil

rosemary, optionally

a pinch of smoked sweet paprika

salt and pepper to taste

*Direction*

1.    Place the chicken breast in a large bowl. Sprinkle it with olive oil, garlic, salt, and pepper. Stir with tongs and let sit for 10 minutes.

2.    Preheat the grill on medium-high to 450-500 °F. Rub with the oiled paper towel.

3.    Place chicken on the grill, close the lid and grill for 8-10 minutes turning once. Don't overcook.

4.    Remove from the grill, cover with foil and let rest for 5 minutes.

## P.M. snack

2 brazil nuts (65 calories)

# Dinner

## Vegan Lasagna

551 calories per person | 4 serves | 1h 20 min

*Ingredients*

1 tbsp olive oil

3/4 cup chopped onion

1 ½ tbsp minced garlic

½ lb cans stewed tomatoes

2 tbsp tomato paste

¼–cup fresh basil

¼ cup parsley

½ tsp salt

½ tsp ground black pepper

½ lb package lasagna noodles

1 lb firm tofu

1 tbsp minced garlic

1/8 cup fresh basil

1/8 cup parsley

¼ tsp salt ground black pepper

5 oz thawed and drained packages frozen chopped spinach


*Direction*

Vegan Lasagna Sauce

1. Take a large heavy saucepan. Heat it over medium heat. Add olive oil.
2. Place the onion in it. Saute the onion until soft about 5 minutes.
3. Add the garlic and cook for 5 minutes.
4. Add the tomatoes and tomato paste.

5. Chop basil, parsley. Add them into the saucepan.
6. Stir the ingredients well. Turn the heat to low. Cook sauce for 1 hour.
7. Salt and pepper.

Main course

1. Boil salted water in a saucepan. Boil the lasagna noodles for 9 minutes in it.
2. Rinse and drain the noodles well.
3. Preheat oven to 400 °F.
4. Place the tofu blocks in a large bowl. Add chopped garlic, basil and parsley, salt and pepper. Mix the ingredients well.
5. Let's assemble the lasagna:
   - Spread 1 cup of sauce in the bottom casserole pan
   - Lay the noodles of lasagna
   - Sprinkle 1/3 tofu mixture over noodles
   - Lay the spinach over the tofu
   - Place 1,5 cup tomato sauce over tofu
   - Place another layer of noodles
   - Sprinkle 1/3 of tofu mixture
   - Top with 1/5 cup tomato sauce
   - Place the final layer of noodles
   - Final 1/3 tofu mixture
   - Spread the remaining tomato
6. Cover the sheet with the foil. Bake lasagna for 30 minutes.

# Week 3 Diet Plan

| MEAL | Week 3 | | | | |
|---|---|---|---|---|---|
| | **Breakfast** | | **Lunch** | **Dinner** | |
| SUNDAY | Avocado Egg Toast | Nuts and Berries Cupcakes | Raw Mushrooms Green Salad | Cucumber Cocktails | Tuna Green and Egg Salad |
| MONDAY | Roasted Veggie Frittata | Tropical Fruit Pudding | Pecan Butter with Brussels Sprouts and Grilled Tuna Steaks | Lemon Berry Cups | Coconut Chicken Strips |
| TUESDAY | Hard-boiled eggs with olives and radish | Dandelion Leaves Green Salad | Boild Chicken breast with Rosemary | Clean Eating Fried Rice with Chicken | Beans and Mushrooms Salad |
| WEDNESDAY | Almond Banana Shake | | Minestrone (slow cooker) | Tuna Green and Egg Salad | |
| THURSDAY | Roll-Up Omelet with Spinach | | Quinoa Enchilada Bake with Cheese | Grilled Salmon with Lemon | Pumpkin Seeds Green Salad |
| FRIDAY | Avocado Chicken Roll | | Quinoa Enchilada Bake with Cheese | Peach Rice Bowl with Shrimp | |
| SATURDAY | Marinara Poached Egg | | Warm Barley Chickpea Tomato Salad | Cauliflower Gratin | Coconut Chicken Strips |

Avocado Egg Toast
Nuts and Berries Cupcakes
Raw Mushrooms Green Salad
Cucumber Cocktails
Tuna Green and Egg Salad
(1195 calories)

# Breakfast

## Avocado Egg Toast

271 calories per person | serves 1 | 15 min

*Ingredients*

¼ avocado

¼ tsp ground pepper

1/8 tsp garlic powder

1 slice toasted whole-wheat bread

1 large boiled egg

1 tbsp sliced scallion

*Direction*

1. Take a small bowl. Combine avocado, garlic, and pepper in it gently.
2. Top the toast with avocado mixture.
3. Cut into half the egg. Place the egg on a top of the toast.
4. If you want to garnish the toast with the scallion.

## A.M. snack

1 medium orange (62 calories)

# Lunch

## Nuts and Berries Cupcakes

300 calories per person | 4 serves | 40 min

*Ingredients*

4 oz peanut butter without any flavoring

2 tbsp cocoa powder

1 chicken egg

1/4 tsp. soda

1/4 tsp vinegar

salt

walnuts, almonds, hazelnuts, pecans (2 tbsp for each kind)

dried or fresh berries (blueberries or cranberries)

*Direction*

1. Preheat oven to 345 °F.
2. In a deep container, place the peanut butter and cocoa powder. Add egg and beat. Add soda, vinegar, and salt. Mix the ingredients using a blender to make a uniform creamy mass.
3. Add nuts or berries in moderation. Fill the cake molds, and place them in the oven. Bake for 15-20 minutes.

## Raw Mushrooms Green Salad

276 calories per person | 1 serves|20 min

*Ingredients*

½ bunch lettuce

4 oz raw champignons

3 ½ walnuts

½-lemon juice

½ tbsp olive oil

salt

*Direction*

1. Place champignons into a colander, and rinse well under running water. Separate the caps from the stems.
2. Put the champignons back in a colander and rinse thoroughly. Allow the mushrooms to dry, then cut them into thin strips and sprinkle with lemon juice.
3. Rinse lettuce leaves well and allow them to dry. After that, break the lettuce into large pieces.
4. Clean nuts, and break into medium pieces. Mix chopped mushrooms, lettuce, and nuts.
5. Season the salad with olive oil, salt, and lemon juice.

# P.M. snack
## Cucumber Cocktails

104 calories per person | 1 serves| 10 min

*Ingredients*

1 cup buttermilk

2 cucumbers

fennel

salt

pepper

*Direction*

1. Finely chop cucumber.
2. Chop the dill. Mix the ingredients with buttermilk.

3. Add salt and pepper to taste. Drink immediately after preparation.

## Dinner

## Tuna Green and Egg Salad

164 calories per person | 1 serves| 20 min
*Ingredients*
3 oz canned tuna
1 oz lettuce
1 chicken eggs
1/4 medium onion
1/2 tbsp olive oil
lemon juice to taste
salt

*Direction*
1. Cut the lettuce and put it on the plate.
2. Open the can and remove the tuna. Cut pieces, if necessary.
3. Mince the onion, and put it on the fish.
4. Boil the eggs. Cut them in half lengthwise.
5. Season the salad with oil. Add a couple drops of lemon juice and salt.

AND

## ¼ medium avocado (80 calories)

Roasted Veggie Frittata
Tropical Fruit Pudding
Pecan Butter with Brussels Sprouts
Grilled Tuna Steaks
Lemon Berry Cups
Coconut Chicken Strips
(1320 calories)

# Breakfast

## Roasted Veggie Frittata

139 calories per person | 1 serves|1h 30 min

*Ingredients*

1/2 medium bell peppers

1/2 garlic clove

1/3 large zucchini

1/6 medium onion

1/6 tbsp olive oil

1 tbsp cup fresh parsley, chopped

1 ½ eggs

1 egg whites

salt to taste

cayenne pepper to taste

2 tbsp finely shredded Parmesan

Nonstick cooking spray

*Direction*

1.   Preheat oven to 400 °F. Place the first oven rack in the lowest position. The second rack must be in the central position in the oven. Line two baking pans with foil. Spray the foil with cooking spray.

2.   Place bell pepper and garlic on one pan. Place zucchini and onion on the other baking pan. Brush the products with olive oil. Place zucchini and onion on the center rack and bake 15 minutes. Remove onion and zucchini.

3.   Place bell pepper and garlic on the lower rack. Roast for 10 minutes.

4. Peel the bell pepper and garlic. Cut pepper into quarters. Cut the zucchini into three 1/2-inch strips. Cut the onion into ½-inch slices. Chop the parsley. Shred the Parmesan.

5. Place the vegetables and garlic in a bowl. Add parsley and ½ tsp of salt.

6. Lower the heat in the oven to the 400 ºF. Coat a 9-x-1.5-inch round cake pan (or smaller) with cooking spray.

7. In a medium bowl, whisk eggs and egg whites. Add remaining salt and cayenne pepper.

8. Add egg mixture to the vegetable mixture. Stir in Parmesan. Place the ingredients into the cake pan.

9. Bake the mixture for 50 minutes.

10. Let the frittata stand 15-30 min before serving.

AND
## Tropical Fruit Pudding
380 calories per person | 2 serves | 35 min
*Ingredients*
1/2 tbsp maple syrup
4 oz silken tofu
1/2 mangos
¼ tsp vanilla extract
a pinch of salt
1/8 tsp salt
1/8 tsp coconut extract
¼ large pineapple, peeled, cored, and quartered
2 tbsp cup unsweetened shredded coconut

*Direction*

1.   Peel, pit, cut into big chunks the mangos. Blend syrup, tofu, mangos, vanilla, salt, and coconut extract in a food processor.   Mix until completely smooth for 1 minute. Transfer the mixture to a large bowl.

2.   Chop pineapple into 1/8-inch pieces, and add to pudding. Cover pudding and refrigerate from 30 minutes up to several hours.

3.   Cook coconut over medium heat in a large skillet. Stir frequently until golden brown, about 5-10 minutes.

4.   Remove coconut from skillet and cool.

5.   Serve the pudding on a plate and sprinkle with coconut.

## A.M. snack

1 medium apple (65 calories)

# Lunch

## Pecan Butter with Brussels sprouts

97 calories per person | 1 serves| 30 min

*Ingredients*

1 cup Brussels sprouts

1/8 cup chopped pecans

½ tbsp Earth Balance (dairy-free butter)

½ tsp brown sugar

¼ tsp lemon juice

Salt to taste

*Direction*

1.  Trim off bottoms of Brussels sprouts. Cut "X" in the bottoms.

2.  Boil water in a large pot. Add salt.

3.  Boil Brussels sprouts for 10 minutes. Drain and place into ice bath sprouts. Cut them in half.

4.  Heat Earth Balance over medium heat.

5.  Add chopped pecans, cook for 2 minutes.

6.  Place the sprouts on the frying pan. Cook over medium-high heat until browned. Brown the other side too.

7.  Add sugar, lemon juice, salt. Combine the ingredients.

8.  Place Brussels on a serving dish. Top them with browned pecans.

AND

# Grilled Tuna Steaks

158 calories per person | 2 serves | 20 min
Ingredients
½ lb raw tuna steaks
1/8 cup chopped fresh parsley
1 sprigs fresh tarragon leaves, removed and chopped
1 clove garlic crushed
1 tsp finely grated lemon zest
sea salt, ground black pepper to taste
½ tbsp extra-virgin olive oil

Direction
Preheat grill or broiler on high. Rinse tuna and pat dry. Set aside.

Combine tarragon, garlic, and lemon peel in a small bowl. Mix well.

Season tuna with salt and pepper. Drizzle with oil; rub rosemary mixture into both sides of tuna. Let rest 5 minutes.

Grill (or broil) tuna for 2 to 5 minutes on each side, or until desired doneness.

AND

# Lemon Berry Cups

118 calories per person | 6 serves | 30 min
*Ingredients*
1 cup fat-free Greek yogurt
½ cup low-fat cream cheese, softened
1 lemon, juice and zest

2 tbsp coconut sugar

¼ cup pecans, chopped

2 large pitted dates

1 cup fresh berries

*Direction*

1.  Beat the yogurt, cream cheese, lemon juice and zest (save a little bit), and coconut sugar until creamy and fluffy.

2.  In small desserts cups, place yogurt, nuts, and berries.

3.  Sprinkle with the pecans and lemon zest before servings.

## P.M. snack

1 medium banana (60 calories)

# Dinner

## Coconut Chicken Strips

261 calories per person | 2 serves |35 min

*Ingredients*

½ lb boneless skinless chicken breasts

1 tbsp extra virgin olive oil

1/8 tsp pepper

¼ tsp salt

½ cup unsweetened coconut flakes (or use shredded coconut

Soy-Ketchup Sauce

¼ cup ketchup

1 tbsp lite soy sauce

1 tbsp water

1/8 tsp pepper

*Direction*

1.    Preheat the oven to 400 °F.

2.    Slice the chicken into strips. Coat the chicken with olive oil.

3.    Mix salt, pepper, and coconut in a bowl. Cover chicken with the mixture.

4.    Place the chicken strips on the baking sheet. Bake for 30 minutes, until golden brown.

5.    Serve the chicken with the sauce.

Sauce –Mix the ingredients in a bowl.

AND

## Cucumber or tomato to taste (6 oz)

Hard-boiled eggs with olives and radish
Dandelion Leaves Green Salad
Boild Chicken breast with Rosemary
Blueberries and Tofu Cheese Smoothies
Clean Eating Fried Rice with Chicken
Beans and Mushrooms Salad
(1340 calories)

# Breakfast

## Hard-boiled eggs with olives and radish

298 calories per person | 2 serves | 15 min

*Ingredients*

2 eggs

10 olives

½ cup radish

avocado oil

salt

pepper

*Direction*

1. Boil two eggs for 10 minutes.
2. Cool, peel and cut them.
3. Drizzle with a little oil of avocado, salt and pepper.
4. Serve the eggs with olives, finely chopped radish.

## A.M. snack

5 pecan halves (50 calories)

# Lunch
## Dandelion Leaves Green Salad
214 calories per person | 1 serves| 1h

*Ingredients*
3 tbsp dandelion leaves
2 leaves sorrel
1 clove of garlic
½ carrot
1 ½ tbsp walnuts
½-lemon juice
½ tbsp olive oil

*Direction*
1. Prepare a deep dish with salted water.
2. Wash and soak dandelion leaves for 30 minutes to get rid of bitterness. Then, remove leaves and allow them to dry. Cut the prepared leaves into medium pieces and place them in a deep bowl.
3. Grind the washed sorrel leaves and add them to the dish.
4. Wash, peel, and grate the carrot and add it to greens.
5. Peel and grind the nuts. Add them to the salad.
6. Clean and crush garlic, then add it to the other ingredients. Mix well.
7. Season the dish with lemon juice and olive oil to taste.

AND

# Boild Chicken breast with Rosemary

265 calories per person| 1 serves|30 min

*Ingredients*

6 oz chicken breast boneless, skinless

rosemary

clove of garlic

salt and pepper to taste

1000 ml water

*Direction*

Take a pan, pour it with water. Add rosemary, garlic.
Place the breast in it. Boil for 15-20 min.
Add salt and pepper for 5 minutes before cooking finish.

# P.M. snack
# Blueberries and Tofu Cheese Smoothies

120 calories per person | 1 serves| 10 min

*Ingredients*

1 cup water

1 cup blueberry

2 oz tofu cheese

1 banana

handful of almonds

*Direction*

1.   Peel and cut the banana into medium slices. Place in a blender.

2.   Add blueberries, tofu and almonds. Add water and beat well.

3. Drink immediately after preparation.

# Dinner
## Fried Rice with Chicken

266 calories per person | 1 serves| 45 min

*Ingredients*

1/4 cup long-grain brown rice

¼-cup water

a pinch of salt

1/6 tbsp olive oil

10 g onions, chopped

1/6 cup diced red or green bell pepper

1/3 boneless skinless chicken breast

1 egg, beaten

½ tbsp soy sauce

1/6 tbsp ginger root, peeled and finely minced

1/3 tsp sesame oil

½ oz scallions (or green onion), chopped

*Direction*

1. Boil water over high heat. Add rice and salt to boiling water. Reduce heat and cover pot. Cook for 30-40 minutes, until liquid is absorbed. Then, remove the rice from the heat. Refrigerate until cold.

2. Add olive oil to a nonstick skillet or wok. Add sliced chicken, bell pepper, onions, and ginger. Cook for 5 minutes over medium heat.

3.   Add rice and remaining water. Cook over medium–high heat.

4.   Push rice to one side of the pan, then add the beaten eggs to the free side. Scramble the dish quickly. Add soy sauce and sesame oil. Cook for 3-4 minutes. Remove skillet from heat.

AND

## Beans and Mushrooms Salad

140 calories per person | 1 serves| 20 min

*Ingredients*

2 oz champignons

3 oz canned beans

1/2 medium pickled cucumber

¼ carrot

1/4 onion

2 tsp olive oil

salt

ground black pepper

*Direction*

1.   Clean and peel the champignons. Cut into medium pieces and fry in olive oil for 10-15 minutes.

2.   Transfer the mushrooms to a bowl to cool.

3.   Clean and mince the onion and grated carrot with a medium grater.

4.   Fry vegetables in olive oil until golden brown. Cool the ingredients.

5. Cut pickled cucumbers into strips and strain the beans through a sieve. If necessary, additionally rinse with water.

6. Finally, take a large dish and combine all ingredients. Salt and pepper the dish to taste.

Almond Banana Shake
Minestrone (slow cooker)
Tuna Green and Egg Salad
Salmon and Asparagus with Onion-Mushroom Sauce
(1373 calories)

# Breakfast
## Almond Banana Shake

405 calories per person | 1 serves|5 min

*Ingredients*

½ cup silken tofu

½ cup milk (1%)

2 bananas

2 tbsp almond butter

2 tbsp hemp seeds

¾ tsp cinnamon

1 tsp vanilla extract

2 tbsp honey

1 cup ice

*Direction*

1.   Place all ingredients in a blender. Do not use ice. Mix well.

2.   Add ice and mix again.

3.   Serve.

# A.M. snack

1/2 medium orange (30 calories)

# Lunch

## Minestrone (slow cooker)

240 calories per person | 1 serves| 3-6h

*Ingredients*

1/6 small onion, diced

1/6 stalk celery, diced

1/3 carrot, peeled and sliced

1/3 zucchini, sliced

1/3 potato, peeled and cubed

1/3 cup green beans (fresh or frozen)

1/6 cup peas (fresh or frozen)

1/3 cup kale, coarsely chopped

1/3 cup vegetable broth or water (for thinner Minestrone)

1/6 can (70 g) diced tomatoes with liquid

1/6 can (70 g) kidney beans, dried and rinsed

20 ml tomato or vegetable juice

1/6 tsp sea salt

a pinch ground black pepper

2 fresh basil leaves, minced

2 tsp Parmesan or Parmigiano Reggiano

*Direction*

1.   Place all the ingredients except kale, parmesan, and basil, in a slow cooker. Cover and cook 5-6 hours on low or 3-4 hours on high.

2.   When the minestrone is cooked, add the kale. Then, cook for 5 minutes on high.

3.   Serve minestrone in the bowls and drizzle with olive oil. Sprinkle the dish with fresh basil and Parmesan.

AND

# Tuna Green and Egg Salad

164 calories per person | 1 serves| 20 min

*Ingredients*

3 oz canned tuna

1 oz lettuce

1 chicken eggs

1/4 medium onion

1/2 tbsp olive oil

lemon juice to taste

salt

*Direction*

1. Cut the lettuce and put it on the plate.
2. Open the can and remove the tuna. Cut pieces, if necessary.
3. Mince the onion, and put it on the fish.
4. Boil the eggs. Cut them in half lengthwise.
5. Season the salad with oil. Add a couple drops of lemon juice and salt.

# P.M. snack

# Cucumber Cocktails

52 caloriesper person | 1 serves| 10 min

*Ingredients*
½ cup buttermilk
1cucumbers
fennel
salt
pepper

*Direction*
1.   Finely chop cucumber.
2.   Chop the dill. Mix the ingredients with buttermilk.
3.   Add salt and pepper to taste. Drink immediately after preparation.

# Dinner
# Salmon and Asparagus with Onion-Mushroom Sauce

478 calories per person | 1 serves| 1h 30 min

*Ingredients*
5 oz salmon (or some other fish)
1 oz champignons
¼ onion
¼ garlic clove
½ tbsp olive oil
2 tsp cup sesame oil
salt
basil
pepper

*Direction*
Marinade
Mix sesame oil with finely chopped garlic, basil, pepper, and salt.
Salmon and Asparagus
1. Cut the salmon, and put into a small saucepan. Pour the marinade over fish and chill in the refrigerator for an hour.
2. Preheat the oven to 355 °F. Cover a baking sheet with foil.
3. Put the slices of salmon and washed asparagus on the baking sheet. Cover them with foil.

4. Bake fish and vegetables in the oven for 15–20 minutes.
5. Wash, peel, and cut champignons. Mince the onion. Fry the ingredients in olive oil until browned.
6. Remove the fish and asparagus from the oven, and top with mushroom and onion mixture. Bake for another 10 minutes.

Roll-Up Omelet with Spinach
Quinoa Enchilada Bake with Cheese
Grilled Salmon with Lemon
Pumpkin Seeds Green Salad
(1296 calories)

# Breakfast
## Roll-Up Omelet with Spinach

198 calories per person | 1 serves| 40 min

*Ingredients*

1 tsp canola oil

1 egg

1 cup baby spinach

1 tsp olive tapenade

1 tbsp crumbled goat cheese

*Direction*

1.    Drizzle canola oil into a nonstick pan. Then, wipe with a paper towel. Heat the pan over medium heat.

2.    Beat egg and swirl into the frying pan. Cook 2 minutes. Then, flip the egg and cook 1 minute.

3.    Carefully place the egg on a plate.

4.    In the same pan, sauté 1 cup of spinach about 1 minute, until wilted.

5.    Top the egg with olive tapenade and goat cheese. Then place wilted spinach on the ingredients.

6.    Roll up the egg and cut in half.

## A.M. snack

1 medium banana (60 calories)

# Lunch
## Quinoa Enchilada Bake with Cheese

407 calories per person | 1 serves| 1 h

*Ingredients*

1/6 cup cooked quinoa

1 oz frozen corn

1 oz tomatoes, finely diced

 1 tbsp black beans, drained

1/8 purple onion, chopped

1 tbsp jalapeno, seeded and diced

1 tbsp Enchilada Sauce

2 oz reduced fat cheddar cheese

2 tsp chopped cilantro

2 tsp black olives, sliced

½ oz avocado, diced

*Direction*

1.  Preheat the oven to 340 °F.

2.  Combine quinoa, corn, one cup of the tomatoes, beans, onions, jalapeno, enchilada sauce, and 1 cup cheddar cheese in a large bowl. Place the ingredients into a 2-quart baking dish.

3.  Top the dish with the remaining cheese. Sprinkle the dish with remaining tomatoes, the cilantro (without 1 tsp), and the sliced olives.

4.  Bake for 50 minutes.

5.  Remove from the oven and top the dish with 1 tsp cilantro and diced avocado. Add salt and pepper to taste.

# P.M. snack 7 almonds (50 calories)

# Dinner
# Grilled Salmon with Lemon

308 calories per serving | 1 serves| 35 min

*Ingredients*

5 oz salmon (or some other fish)

¼ lemon

½ tbsp extra virgin olive oil

¼ tbsp fresh squeezed lemon juice

1 tbsp fresh rosemary, minced

¼ tbsp Dijon mustard

1/2 clove garlic, minced

sea salt and black pepper to taste

1 bamboo or wood skewers, soaked in warm water for 30 minutes

*Direction*

1.   Heat the grill on medium heat. Spray the grates with olive oil.

2.   Mix oregano, lemon juice, mustard, fresh rosemary, garlic, and black pepper in a bowl.

3.   Cut salmon into cubes.

4.   Slice the lemon into thin rings.

5.   Thread salmon and lemon slices onto the skewers, alternating between salmon and lemon. You should have about eight pairs.

6.   Spray the kebobs with oil, spice mixture, and salt.

7. Grill the fish and lemon about 10 minutes, turning occasionally.

AND
## Pumpkin Seeds Green Salad

273 calories per person |1 serves|20 min

*Ingredients*
1 cups mixture of lettuce leaves
1 oz dried pumpkin seeds
2 oz ceps
pumpkin oil
½ tbsp olive oil
salt

*Direction*
1. Peel the pumpkin seeds and fry them in preheated olive oil until they crackle.
2. Transfer them to a deep plate.
3. Wash, clean and cut the mushrooms into slices. Fry for 3-5 minutes in olive oil.
4. Combine mushrooms with the seeds.
5. Wash, dry and shred lettuce leaves. Add leaves to seeds and mushrooms. Mix well and season with salt and pumpkin oil.

Avocado Chicken Roll
Quinoa Enchilada Bake with Cheese
Peach Rice Bowl with Shrimp
(1322 calories)

# Breakfast
## Avocado Chicken Roll

397 calories per person | 1 serves| 15 min

*Ingredients*

4 oz fried chicken breast

1 tbsp olive oil

½ medium avocado, 3 oz

salt

pepper

*Direction*

1. Cut the chicken into thin long strips.
2. Cut avocado into medium slices, put them in a plate, and mix with olive oil and salt and pepper to taste.
3. Put avocado mixture on the meat strips. Roll strips.

# A.M. snack

1 medium apple (65 calories)

# Lunch

## Quinoa Enchilada Bake with Cheese

407 calories per person | 1 serves| 1h

*Ingredients*

1/6 cup cooked quinoa

1 oz frozen corn

1 oz tomatoes, finely diced

½ oz black beans, drained

1/8 purple onion, chopped

1 tbsp jalapeno, seeded and diced

1 tbsp Enchilada Sauce

2 oz reduced fat cheddar cheese

2 tsp chopped cilantro

2 tsp black olives, sliced

½ oz avocado, diced

*Direction*

1.    Preheat the oven to 340 °F.

2.    Combine quinoa, corn, one cup of the tomatoes, beans, onions, jalapeno, enchilada sauce, and 1 cup cheddar cheese in a large bowl. Place the ingredients into a 2-quart baking dish.

3.    Top the dish with the remaining cheese. Sprinkle the dish with remaining tomatoes, the cilantro (without 1 tsp), and the sliced olives.

4.    Bake for 50 minutes.

5.    Remove from the oven and top the dish with 1 tsp cilantro and diced avocado. Add salt and pepper to taste.

# P.M. snack 5 pecan halves (50 calories)
# Dinner
# Peach Rice Bowl with Shrimp

403 calories per person | 1 serves| 40 min

*Ingredients*
¾ cup uncooked brown rice
1 ½ low-sodium chicken broth (or use vegetable broth)
120 g shelled large raw shrimp
1/2 firm, ripe peach, pitted and chopped
¼ clove garlic, peeled and sliced
a pinch of saffron threads (optional)
a pinch of paprika
a pinch of sea salt
¼ tbsp fresh lime juice
1 oz cilantro leaves, coarsely chopped
½ tbsp extra virgin olive oil
¼ lime, cut into 4 wedges

*Direction*
1.   Add the broth and rice to a pot and bring to a boil. Cover the pot and cook for 35 minutes, until liquid is absorbed and rice is tender. Fluff with a fork.

2.   Toss chopped peaches with a half of lime juice. Set aside.

3.   Heat sauté pan over medium heat. Add olive oil, then shrimp, salt to taste, paprika, cayenne pepper, and saffron. Cook for 3 minutes.

4. Add garlic. Cook for 1 minute, until shrimp are pink and opaque. Then, remove the pan from heat.

5. Remove the rice to a bowl. Add shrimp and peaches and sprinkle the dish with the cilantro.

6. Serve with lemon wedges if desired.

Marinara Poached Egg
Warm Barley Chickpea Tomato Salad
Cauliflower Gratin
Coconut Chicken Strips
(1236 calories)

# Breakfast
## Marinara Poached Egg
306 calories per person | 1 serves| 15 min

*Ingredients*
2 tsp olive oil
¼ small yellow onion
A pinch of red pepper flakes
½ cup marinara sauce
1 egg
1 small whole wheat pita pocket

*Direction*
1.   Heat the olive oil in a small sauté pan over medium heat.
2.   Sauté the onion in the pan until brown, approximately 5 minutes.
3.   Add red pepper flakes and marinara sauce. Cook about 1 minute.
4.   Gently break the egg into the pan. Cover the pan and simmer about 5 to 7 minutes until egg white is firm.
5.   Serve the dish with pita pocket. You can toast it and tear it into wedges.

## A.M. snack
1 medium orange (62 calories)

# Lunch

## Warm Barley Chickpea Tomato Salad

402 calories per person | 1 serves| 45 min

*Ingredients*

1/8 cup uncooked barley

3 oz chicken fillet

1/4 tbsp extra virgin olive oil

1/8 cup cherry tomatoes, halved

1/4 cup pre-cooked chickpeas

¼ bunch of fresh sage

1/8 tbsp balsamic vinegar

salt and pepper to taste

*Direction*

1.   Bring the barley to a boil in a pot with salted water. Then, cover and simmer on low heat for ½ hour, until tender.

2.   Drain and rinse barley. Set aside.

3.   Heat griddle to medium. Grill the chicken for 2 minutes per side. If chicken is thick, it may need to cook longer. Then, chop and set aside.

4.   Sauté the tomatoes in a saucepan with olive oil over medium heat. Cook for 1 minute.

5.   Add chickpeas, barley, and sage to tomatoes. Stir the ingredients for 5 minutes.

6.   Add the chicken. Cook for 1-2 minutes.

7.   Season the dish with balsamic vinegar, salt and pepper to taste. Cook for 1 minute.

8.   Eat warm.

## P.M. snack

1 medium apple (65 calories)

## Dinner
## Cauliflower Gratin

140 calories per person | 4 serves | 50 min

*Ingredients*

1 ½ lb cauliflower

1 tbsp vegan butter

1 tbsp chickpea flour

1 cups cashew milk

1/4 tsp kosher salt

black pepper to taste

Nutmeg, a pinch

¼ cup vegan cheddar cheese

2 tbsp gluten-free bread crumbs

1 tbsp vegan grated parmesan

1 tbsp extra-virgin olive oil

*Direction*

1.   Wash and cut into large florets the cauliflower.

2.   Boil water in a pot a few minutes. Place the florets in it. Blanche the cauliflower until tendering but with crunch.

3.   Drain and rinse the cauliflower with cold water.

4.   Preheat the oven to 400 °F.

5.   Melt the butter in a medium-size saucepan. Add the flour until well combined.

6.   Add the warm milk. Whisk milk until a smooth sauce.

7. Salt and pepper. Add the nutmeg, cheese. Whisk the ingredients until smooth. Turn off the heat.

8. Put a part of the béchamel sauce in the bottom of baking sheet (8x8-inch).

9. Combine the breadcrumbs, oil and parmesan. Mix them. Sprinkle them over the cauliflower.

10. Bake for 30 minutes. Turn the oven on broiler for a few minutes for crisp up the top.

AND

# Coconut Chicken Strips

261 calories per person | 4 serves | 35 min

*Ingredients*

1 lb boneless skinless chicken breasts

2 tbsp extra virgin olive oil

¼ tsp pepper

½ tsp salt

1 cup unsweetened coconut flakes (or use shredded coconut

Soy-Ketchup Sauce

½ cup ketchup

2 tbsp lite soy sauce

2 tbsp water

¼ tsp pepper

*Direction*

1. Preheat the oven to 200 ºC.

2. Slice the chicken into strips. Coat the chicken with olive oil.

3. Mix salt, pepper, and coconut in a bowl. Cover chicken with the mixture.

4. Place the chicken strips on the baking sheet. Bake for 30 minutes, until golden brown.

5. Serve the chicken with the sauce.

Sauce

Mix the ingredients in a bowl.

# Calorie Chart

## Fruits Calories

| Food | Serving | Calories | Food | Serving | Calories |
|------|---------|----------|------|---------|----------|
| Acai | 1 oz. (28.35 g) | 20 | Mandarin Oranges | 1 mandarin orange (88 g) | 47 |
| Apple | 1 apple (182 g) | 95 | Mango | 1 mango (336 g) | 202 |
| Applesauce | 1 cup (246 g) | 167 | Minneola | 1 minneola (109 g) | 70 |
| Apricot | 1 apricot (35 g) | 17 | Mulberries | 1 cup (140 g) | 60 |
| Avocado | 1 avocado (200 g) | 320 | Nectarine | 1 nectarine (150 g) | 66 |
| Banana | 1 banana (125 g) | 111 | Olives | 1 olive (2.7 g) | 2 |
| Blackberries | 1 cup (144 g) | 62 | Orange | 1 orange (131 g) | 62 |
| Blood Oranges | 1 serving (140 g) | 70 | Papaya | 1 fruit (500 g) | 215 |
| Blueberries | 1 cup (148 g) | 84 | Passion Fruit | 1 passoin fruit (18 g) | 17 |
| Cantaloupe | 1 wedge (69 g) | 23 | Peach | 1 peach (150 g) | 59 |
| Cherries | 1 cherry (8 g) | 4 | Pear | 1 pear (178 g) | 101 |
| Clementine | 1 clementine (74 g) | 35 | Persimmon | 1 fruit (25 g) | 32 |
| Cranberries | 1 cup (100 g) | 46 | Physalis | 1 berry (5 g) | 2 |
| Currants | 1 cup (112 g) | 63 | Pineapple | 1 pineapple (905 g) | 453 |
| Custard Apple | 1 custard apple (135 g) | 136 | Plantains | 1 plantain (179 g) | 218 |
| Dates | 1 date (7.1 g) | 20 | Plum | 1 plum (66 g) | 30 |
| Figs | 1 fig (50 g) | 37 | Pomegranate | 1 pomegranate (282 g) | 234 |
| Fruit salad | 1 cup (249 g) | 125 | Quince | 1 quince (92 g) | 52 |
| Grapes | 1 cup (151 g) | 104 | Raisins | 1 cup (145 g) | 434 |
| Greengage | 1 fruit (5 g) | 2 | Rambutan | 1 rambutan (9 g) | 7 |
| Guava | 1 guava (55 g) | 37 | Raspberries | 1 cup (123 g) | 64 |
| Jackfruit | 1 cup (151 g) | 143 | Rhubarb | 1 stalk (51 g) | 11 |
| Jujube | 1 oz. (28.35 g) | 22 | Starfruit | 1 star fruit (91 g) | 28 |
| Kiwi | 1 liwi (183 g) | 112 | Strawberries | 1 cup (152 g) | 49 |
| Lemon | 1 lemon (58 g) | 17 | Tamarind | 1 tamarind (2 g) | 5 |
| Lime | 1 lime (67 g) | 20 | Tangerine | 1 tangerine (88 g) | 47 |
| Lychees | 1 lychee (10 g) | 7 | Watermelon | 1 wedge (286 g) | 86 |

# Vegetables Calories

| Food | Serving | Calories |
|---|---|---|
| Artichoke | 1 artichoke (128 g) | 60 |
| Arugula | 1 leaf (2 g) | 1 |
| Asparagus | 1 spear (12 g) | 2 |
| Aubergine | 1 aubergine (458 g) | 115 |
| Beetroot | 1 beet (82 g) | 35 |
| Bell Pepper | 1 pepper (73 g) | 15 |
| Black Olives | 1 olive (2.7 g) | 2 |
| Broccoli | 1 bunch (608 g) | 207 |
| Brussels Sprouts | 1 sprout (19 g) | 8 |
| Cabbage | 1 head (908 g) | 227 |
| Capsicum | 1 pepper (45 g) | 12 |
| Carrot | 1 carrot (61 g) | 25 |
| Cauliflower | 1 floweret (13 g) | 3 |
| Celery | 1 stalk (40 g) | 6 |
| Chard | 1 leaf (48 g) | 9 |
| Cherry Tomato | 1 cherry tomato (20 g) | 20 |
| Chicory | 1 head (53 g) | 38 |
| Chinese Cabbage | 1 head (840 g) | 134 |
| Chives | 1 tbsp, chopped (3 g) | 1 |
| Collard Greens | 1 cup, raw (36 g) | 12 |
| Corn | 1 cup (154 g) | 562 |
| Courgette | 1 courgette (196 g) | 33 |
| Creamed Spinach | 1 cup (200 g) | 148 |
| Cucumber | 1 cucumber (410 g) | 66 |
| Eggplant | 1 eggplant (458 g) | 115 |
| Endive | 1 head (513 g) | 87 |
| Fennel | 1 bulb (234 g) | 73 |
| Garlic | 1 clove (3 g) | 4 |
| Gherkin | 1 gherkin (65 g) | 9 |
| Gourd | 1 gourd (771 g) | 108 |
| Green Beans | 1 cup (110 g) | 34 |

| Food | Serving | Calories |
|---|---|---|
| Green Olives | 1 olive (2.7 g) | 2 |
| Green Onion | 1 green onion (15 g) | 5 |
| Horseradish | 1 tbsp (15 g) | 7 |
| Kale | 1 cup, chopped (67 g) | 33 |
| Kohlrabi | 1 kohlrabi (400 g) | 108 |
| Kumara | 1 kumara (130 g) | 112 |
| Leek | 1 leek (89 g) | 54 |
| Lettuce | 1 head (600 g) | 90 |
| Mushrooms | 1 mushroom (5.4 g) | 1 |
| Mustard Greens | 1 cup, chopped (56 g) | 15 |
| Nori | 1 sheet (2.6 g) | 1 |
| Okra | 1 pod (12 g) | 4 |
| Olives | 1 olive (2.7 g) | 2 |
| Onion | 1 onion (85 g) | 34 |
| Parsnips | 1 parsnip (170 g) | 128 |
| Peas | 1 cup (98 g) | 79 |
| Pepper | 1 pepper (75 g) | 20 |
| Potato | 1 potato (213 g) | 164 |
| Pumpkin | 1 pumpkin (196 g) | 51 |
| Radishes | 1 radish (4.5 g) | 1 |
| Red Cabbage | 1 leaf (22 g) | 7 |
| Rutabaga | 1 rutabaga (386 g) | 147 |
| Shallots | 1 shallot (25 g) | 18 |
| Spinach | 1 bunch (340 g) | 78 |
| Squash | 1 squash (196 g) | 88 |
| Sweet Potato | 1 potato (130 g) | 112 |
| Tomato | 1 tomato (111 g) | 20 |
| Turnip Greens | 1 turnip green (170 g) | 34 |
| Turnips | 1 turnip (122 g) | 34 |
| Wasabi | 1 root (169 g) | 184 |
| Zucchini | 1 zucchini (196 g) | 33 |

# Cheese Calories

| Cheese | Serving | Calories | Cheese | Serving | Calories |
|---|---|---|---|---|---|
| American Cheese | 1 slice (21 g) | 31 | Gruyere | 1 slice (25 g) | 103 |
| Applewood | 1 slice (20 g) | 82 | Halloumi | 1 oz. (28.35 g) | 90 |
| Asiago Cheese | 1 oz. (28.35 g) | 110 | Havarti | 1 slice (28 g) | 104 |
| Babybel | 1 piece (21 g) | 70 | Italian Cheese | 1 serving (30 g) | 119 |
| Blue Cheese | 1 oz. (28.35 g) | 99 | Jarlsberg | 1 oz. (28.35 g) | 99 |
| Brie | 1 slice (30 g) | 100 | Maasdam Cheese | 1 slice (18 g) | 62 |
| Camembert | 1 slice (30 g) | 90 | Manchego Cheese | 1 serving (28 g) | 90 |
| Cheddar | 1 slice (22 g) | 89 | Monterey | 1 cup (132 g) | 492 |
| Cheese Fondue | 1 packet (400 g) | 912 | Monterey Jack Cheese | 1 cup (132 g) | 492 |
| Cheese Spread | 1 tbsp (15 g) | 44 | Mozzarella | 1 slice (28 g) | 78 |
| Cheese Whiz | 1 tbsp (33 g) | 91 | Muenster Cheese | 1 slice (28 g) | 103 |
| Chester | 1 oz. (28.35 g) | 108 | Neufchatel | 1 package (85 g) | 215 |
| Colby Cheese | 1 cup (132 g) | 520 | Parmesan | 1 tsp (5 g) | 22 |
| Colby-Jack Cheese | 1 cup (132 g) | 520 | Pecorino | 1 tbsp (5 g) | 19 |
| Cottage Cheese | 1 cup (210 g) | 206 | Provolone | 1 slice (28 g) | 98 |
| Dutch Cheese | 1 oz. (28.35 g) | 110 | Raclette Cheese | 1 slice (25 g) | 89 |
| Edam Cheese | 1 package (198 g) | 707 | Ricotta | 1 cup (246 g) | 428 |
| Emmentaler | 1 slice (25 g) | 89 | Romano | 5 package (142 g) | 550 |
| Feta | 1 oz. (28.35 g) | 74 | Roquefort | 1 oz. (28.35 g) | 103 |
| Fontina | 1 slice (30 g) | 117 | Sheep Cheese | 1 oz. (28.35 g) | 102 |
| Fresh Mozzarella | 1 slice (28 g) | 78 | Soft Cheese | 1 oz. (28.35 g) | 75 |
| Gjetost | 1 package (227 g) | 1058 | Stilton Cheese | 1 oz. (28.35 g) | 110 |
| Goat Cheese | 1 oz. (28.35 g) | 102 | String Cheese | 1 stick (28 g) | 70 |
| Gorgonzola | 1 oz. (28.35 g) | 98 | Swiss Cheese | 1 slice (25 g) | 95 |
| Gouda | 1 package (198 g) | 705 | White Cheddar | 1 cup (132 g) | 532 |
| Grated Parmesan | 1 tsp (5 g) | 22 | Wisconsin Cheese | 1 oz. (28.35 g) | 109 |

# Milk & Dairy Products Calories

| Food | Serving | Calories |
|---|---|---|
| Almond Milk | 1 cup (235 g) | 40 |
| Buttermilk | 1 cup (254 g) | 157 |
| Chocolate Mousse | 1/2 cup (202 g) | 455 |
| Coconut Milk | 1 cup (240 g) | 552 |
| Coffee Creamer | 1 tbsp (15 g) | 29 |
| Condensed Milk | 1 cup (306 g) | 982 |
| Cottage Cheese | 1 cup (210 g) | 206 |
| Cream | 1 tbsp (15 g) | 36 |
| Creme Fraiche | 1 tbsp (14 g) | 55 |
| Curd | 1 cup (210 g) | 206 |
| Custard | 1/2 cup (141 g) | 172 |
| Evaporated Milk | 1 cup (252 g) | 340 |
| Goat Milk | 1 cup (244 g) | 168 |
| Hot Chocolate | 1 cup (266 g) | 237 |
| Kefir | 1 cup (246 g) | 135 |
| Lactose-free Milk | 1 cup (250 g) | 130 |
| Lassi | 1 glass (200 g) | 150 |
| Milk | 1 cup (244 g) | 149 |
| Plain Yogurt | 1 container (227 g) | 138 |
| Powdered Milk | 1 cup (68 g) | 337 |
| Quark | 1 cup (220 g) | 319 |
| Rice Milk | 1 cup (245 g) | 120 |
| Rice Pudding | 1 serving (113 g) | 133 |
| Semi-skimmed Milk | 1 serving (250 g) | 125 |
| Semolina Pudding | 1 serving (143 g) | 96 |
| Skim Milk | 1 cup (247 g) | 86 |
| Sour Cream | 1 tbsp (12 g) | 22 |
| Soy Milk | 1 cup (243 g) | 109 |
| Sweetened Condensed Milk | 1 cup (306 g) | 982 |
| Tzatziki | 1 tbsp (15 g) | 18 |
| Whipped Cream | 1 tbsp (3 g) | 8 |
| Whole Milk | 1 cup (244 g) | 149 |
| Yogurt | 1 container (227 g) | 138 |

# Meta Calories

| Food | Serving | Calories |
|------|---------|----------|
| Alligator | 1 serving (153 g) | 355 |
| Beef | 1 steak (164 g) | 407 |
| Beef Brisket | 1 piece (1780 g) | 4308 |
| Beef Jerky | 1 piece (20 g) | 82 |
| Beef Ribs | 1 piece (225 g) | 536 |
| Beef Tenderloin | 1 steak (140 g) | 305 |
| Chicken | 1/2 chicken (334 g) | 731 |
| Chicken Breast | 1 breast (200 g) | 344 |
| Chicken Drumstick | 1 drumstick (71 g) | 131 |
| Chicken Fat | 1 cup (205 g) | 1841 |
| Chicken Giblets | 1 cup (145 g) | 229 |
| Chicken Gizzards | 1 cup (145 g) | 212 |
| Chicken Leg | 1 leg (199 g) | 346 |
| Chicken Liver | 1 liver (44 g) | 73 |
| Chicken Meat | 1 breast (200 g) | 344 |
| Chicken Thigh | 1 thigh (111 g) | 254 |
| Chicken Wing | 1 wing (29 g) | 77 |
| Chuck Steak | 1 steak (310 g) | 859 |
| Cubed Steak | 1 serving (165 g) | 328 |
| Duck | 1/2 duck (634 g) | 2137 |
| Filet Mignon | 1 fillet (104 g) | 278 |
| Flank Steak | 1 steak (188 g) | 365 |
| Flat Iron Steak | 1 steak (252 g) | 345 |

| Food | Serving | Calories |
|------|---------|----------|
| Ground Beef | 1 patty (70 g) | 172 |
| Ground Round | 1 piece (113 g) | 278 |
| Ham | 1 slice (145 g) | 236 |
| New York Strip Steak | 1 steak (214 g) | 426 |
| Ostrich | 1 serving (85 g) | 123 |
| Pork | 1 chop (185 g) | 363 |
| Pork Baby Back Ribs | 1 rib (70 g) | 148 |
| Pork Chops | 1 chop (131 g) | 257 |
| Pork Country-Style Ribs | 1 rib (60 g) | 148 |
| Pork Loin | 1 chop (83 g) | 169 |
| Pork Roast | 1 roast (830 g) | 2108 |
| Pork Steaks | 1 steak (264 g) | 517 |
| Roast Beef | 1 roast (515 g) | 721 |
| Round Steak | 1 steak (236 g) | 430 |
| Schnitzel | 1 schnitzel (130 g) | 203 |
| Spare Ribs | 1 rack (1400 g) | 3332 |
| Standing Rib Roast | 1 serving (113 g) | 376 |
| T-Bone Steak | 1 steak (287 g) | 580 |
| Turkey | 1 turkey (3812 g) | 7205 |
| Turkey Breast | 1/2 breast (864 g) | 1166 |
| Turkey Legs | 1 leg (546 g) | 1136 |
| Turkey Steak | 1 steak (170 g) | 321 |
| Turkey Wings | 1 wing (24 g) | 53 |

# Non-Alcoholic Drinks & Beverage

| Food | Serving | Calories |
|------|---------|----------|
| ACE Drink | 1/2 litre (500 ml) | 220 |
| Apple Spritzer | 1/2 litre (500 ml) | 120 |
| Chai | 1 cup (236 ml) | 0 |
| Chai Tea | 1 cup (236 ml) | 0 |
| Chocolate Milk | 1 cup (266 ml) | 237 |
| Chocolate Milkshake | 10 fl. oz. (283 ml) | 354 |
| Club Mate | 1/2 litre (500 ml) | 150 |
| Coca Cola | 1 can (330 ml) | 139 |
| Coffee | 1 cup (237 ml) | 2 |
| Coke Zero | 1 can (330 ml) | 3 |
| Cola | 1 can (330 ml) | 139 |
| Crystal Light | 8 fl. oz. (237 ml) | 623 |
| Diet Coke | 1 can (330 ml) | 3 |
| Egg Cream | 1 serving (125 ml) | 118 |
| Egg Nog | 1 cup (254 ml) | 224 |
| Elderflower Cordial | 8 oz. (227 ml) | 66 |
| Evian | 1 bottle (500 ml) | 0 |
| Gatorade | 12 fl. oz. (355 ml) | 82 |
| Ginger Tea | 1 cup (254 ml) | 0 |
| Hawaiian Punch | 8 oz. (227 ml) | 70 |
| Hi-C | 12 fl. oz. (253 ml) | 124 |
| Horchata | 8 fl. oz. (240 ml) | 130 |
| Hot Chocolate | 1 cup (266 ml) | 237 |
| Ice Tea | 12 fl. oz. (355 ml) | 96 |
| Iced Tea | 12 fl. oz. (355 ml) | 96 |

| Food | Serving | Calories |
|------|---------|----------|
| Kombucha | 8 oz. (227 ml) | 30 |
| Kool-Aid | 8 fl. oz. (237 ml) | 62 |
| Lassi | 1 cup (250 ml) | 260 |
| Latte Macchiato | 1 cup (300 ml) | 171 |
| Lemonade | 12 fl. oz. (355 ml) | 149 |
| Malt Beer | 1 cup (237 ml) | 88 |
| Milk | 1 cup (244 ml) | 149 |
| Milkshake (dry) | 1 tbsp (7 ml) | 23 |
| Milo | 3 tbsp (24 ml) | 98 |
| Nectar | 8 oz. (227 ml) | 120 |
| Nestea | 1 cup (240 ml) | 86 |
| Non-alcoholic Beer | 1 can, bottle (354 ml) | 131 |
| Powerade | 1 bottle (500 ml) | 80 |
| Slurpee | 8 oz. (240 ml) | 10 |
| Slush Puppie | 8 fl. oz. (237 ml) | 119 |
| Smoothie | 8 oz. (240 ml) | 89 |
| Soy Milk | 1 cup (243 ml) | 109 |
| Strawberry Milkshake | 10 fl. oz. (283 ml) | 320 |
| Tang | 1/8 cap (24 ml) | 91 |
| Tap Water | 1 fl. oz. (29.6 ml) | 0 |
| Tea | 1 cup (237 ml) | 2 |
| Vanilla Milkshake | 10 fl. oz. (283 ml) | 422 |
| Volvic | 1/2 litre (500 ml) | 0 |
| Water | 1 fl. oz. (29.6 ml) | 0 |
| Yerba Mate | 1 serving (50 ml) | 31 |

# Nuts & Seeds Calories

| Food | Serving | Calories |
|---|---|---|
| Acorn | 1 oz. (28.35 g) | 108 |
| Alfalfa Sprouts | 1 cup (33 g) | 8 |
| Almonds | 1 cup (95 g) | 546 |
| Beechnut | 1 oz. (28.35 g) | 161 |
| Brazil Nuts | 1 cup (133 g) | 872 |
| Breadfruit | 1 oz. (28.35 g) | 53 |
| Butternut | 1 cup (120 g) | 734 |
| Cashew | 1 oz. (28.35 g) | 155 |
| Chestnut | 1 cup (145 g) | 309 |
| Chia Seeds | 1 oz. (28.35 g) | 136 |
| Coconut | 1 coconut (397 g) | 1405 |
| Cotton Seeds | 1 cup (149 g) | 754 |
| Flaxseed | 1 cup (168 g) | 897 |
| Ginkgo Nuts | 1 oz. (28.35 g) | 51 |
| Goa Bean | 1 cup (182 g) | 744 |
| Hazelnut | 1 cup (75 g) | 471 |
| Hickory Nuts | 1 cup (120 g) | 788 |
| Lima Beans | 1/2 cup (124 g) | 88 |
| Lotus Seed | 1 oz. (28.35 g) | 25 |
| Macadamia Nuts | 1 cup (134 g) | 962 |
| Peanuts | 1 cup (146 g) | 828 |
| Peas | 1 cup (145 g) | 117 |
| Pecan Nuts | 1 cup (99 g) | 684 |
| Pecans | 1 cup (99 g) | 684 |
| Pili Nuts | 1 cup (120 g) | 863 |
| Pine Nuts | 1 cup (135 g) | 909 |
| Pinto Beans | 1 cup (193 g) | 670 |
| Pistachios | 1 cup (123 g) | 691 |
| Poppy Seeds | 1 tbsp (8.8 g) | 42 |
| Pumpkin Seeds | 1 cup (129 g) | 721 |
| Radish Seeds | 1 cup (38 g) | 16 |
| Safflower Seeds | 1 oz. (28.35 g) | 145 |
| Sesame Seeds | 1 cup (144 g) | 825 |
| Smoked Almonds | 1 cup (95 g) | 546 |
| Soy Beans | 1 cup (256 g) | 376 |
| Sunflower Seeds | 1 cup (140 g) | 818 |
| Sweet Chestnut | 1 oz. (28.35 g) | 54 |
| Walnuts | 1 cup (80 g) | 523 |
| Watermelon | 1 wedge (286 g) | 86 |

Thank you for spending three weeks with us. We hope that it was tasty, and you have a new habit of healthy eating. Leave your feedback and suggestions, because we want to become better with you.


Karla Bro

Made in the USA
Columbia, SC
09 March 2020